WHEATON PRESS
READ. RESPOND. REFLECT.

MESSIAH
INVITED TO FOLLOW

Life of Christ
Student Guide 200
Published by Wheaton Press © 2010, 2019
Wheaton, Illinois

www.WheatonPress.com

ISBN-13: 978-1-950258-03-1
ISBN-10: 1-950258-03-3

1. Christian Education – Discipleship 2. Spiritual Formation – Discipleship. 3. Culture & Theology – Education. 4. Nonfiction-Religion and Spirituality-Christian Life. 5. Nonfiction-Spiritual Growth-Christ-centered.

Copyright and Trademark Standard

Accordingly, international and domestic laws and penalties guaranteeing patent, copyright, trademark, and trade secret protection safeguard the ideas, concepts, and recommendations related within this document.

Contact the publisher for discounted copies for partner schools and receive free resources and training for teachers.

Learn more at WheatonPress.com or email WheatonPress@gmail.com

Equipping Students to Reflect Christ

	STEP ONE	STEP TWO	STEP THREE	STEP FOUR
Growth Emphasis	An Emphasis on Believing	An Emphasis on Following	An Emphasis on Loving	An Emphasis on Going
Essential Questions	1. What does a healthy, mature follower of Christ believe? 2. How does a healthy, mature follower of Christ live?	3. How do I grow as a healthy, mature follower of Christ? 4. How do I equip others to grow as healthy, mature followers of Christ?	5. Who do others say Jesus is? 6. Who do I say Jesus is?	7. How will I reflect and steward my unique gifts? 8. Where is my circle of influence?
Essential Outcomes	Understand and articulate Christ-centered beliefs	Develop authentic Christ-centered values	Develop and articulate a Christ-centered mission	Develop a clear Christ-centered personal vision
Courses	Foundation of Faith I Foundation of Faith II	Life of Christ Spiritual Formation	Philosophy & Theology Doctrine & Apologetics	Leadership, Evangelism, & Discipleship Christ & Culture
Leadership Pipeline	D Groups	MENTOR PROJECT	LEADERSHIP INSTITUTE	The Glory Project

Essential Questions

1 Who is Jesus?
2 What is my response to His invitation?

Unit Essential Questions

1 Jesus: Who do others say that He is?

2 Perspective: How do I view Jesus?

3 Messiah: Is Jesus the Messiah?

4 Divine: Is Jesus fully God?

5 Human: Was Jesus fully human?

6 Atonement: Why did Jesus die on a cross?

7 Risen: Did Jesus rise from the dead?

8 Return: What will happen when Jesus returns?

9 Respond: Who do I say that He is?

Course Description

This class will focus on inviting students to become friends of Christ. Students will examine and apply the concept of Christ's role as our prophet, priest, and king. Students will gain an understanding of Jesus as the fulfillment of prophecy and will not only understand His place in history, but also His relevance to our lives today. Ultimately, the hope is that Jesus' life and message will transform students' lives as they gain a greater understanding of who Christ is in their individual lives and personalize their response to Him.

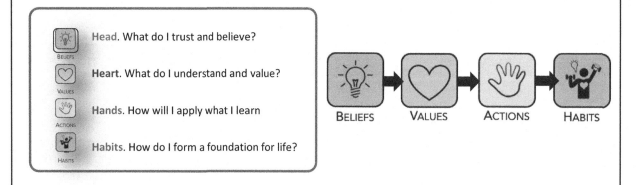

Head. What do I trust and believe?

Heart. What do I understand and value?

Hands. How will I apply what I learn

Habits. How do I form a foundation for life?

BELIEFS   VALUES   ACTIONS   HABITS

Course Overview

The purpose of this course is to equip students with basic guidelines, principles, and tools to effectively evaluate the claims, sources, and accounts of Jesus of Nazareth. Students will be invited to assess Biblical, historical non-Christian, and contemporary non-Christian sources to construct a personal trustworthy and reliable lens to determine their response to the man, myth, legend, or Messiah known as Jesus Christ.

Learning Outcomes

A   Jesus is our prophet, priest, and king.

B   Jesus is 100% fully God and 100% fully human (hypostatic union).

C   Jesus is—and claimed to be—the only God (Christian theism, Trinity).

D   Jesus lived a sinless life (incarnation).

E   Jesus became the penal substitutionary atonement for our sin (justification).

F   Jesus rose from the dead and is currently sitting at the right hand of the Father as our mediator and intercessor in His exalted Glory (Christology).

G   Jesus will return (eschatology).

H   Jesus invites us into relationship with Him and to follow Him in discipleship (soteriology, sanctification, missiology).

They went to Capernaum, and when the Sabbath came, Jesus went into the synagogue and began to teach.

Mark 1:17

Course Overview

Unit 1	Who is Jesus?
1	What is the learning goal for this workbook, The Life of Christ?
2	What do I currently know about Jesus?
3	What is the Gospel Project?
4	What is the context for the essential question for this class?
5	What does John 1–2 reveal about Christ?
6	How does our culture view Christ?

Unit 2	Perspective: How do I view Jesus?
1	What is the tri–perspective view of Jesus?
2	How does my perspective of Jesus influence my relationship with Him?
3	What is the application of the tri–perspective view of Christ to my life?
4	What does John 3–8 reveal about Christ?
5	What are the faith foundations of a complete monist?

Unit 3	Messiah: Is Jesus the Messiah?
1	What does the Bible tell us about the Messiah?
2	Does Jesus meet the requirements to be the Messiah?
3	How does the central theme of Scripture center on Christ?
4	What does John 9–15 reveal about Jesus?

Unit 4	Divine: Is Jesus fully God?
1	Why would it matter whether or not Jesus was fully Divine?
2	What do other religions believe about the divinity of Jesus Christ?
3	Did Jesus claim to be God?
4	Why was Jesus crucified?
5	What is significant about the word Elohim?
6	What does John 16–21 reveal about Christ?

Unit 5	Human: Was Jesus fully human?
1	Was Jesus fully human?
2	What is Gnosticism?
3	What is the kenosis, and why does it matter?
4	If Jesus was fully human, how could he live a perfect life?
5	What does Matthew 1–7 reveal about Jesus?

Unit 6	Atonement: Why did Jesus die?
1	What happened physically to Christ on the cross?
2	What happened spiritually through the sacrifice of Christ on the cross?
3	What happened theologically through the atoning work of Christ?
4	How are the perfect love and perfect wrath of God fulfilled through the death of Christ on the cross?
5	Did Jesus go to hell after He died?

Course Overview

Unit 7	Resurrected: Did Jesus rise from the dead?
1	What do I believe about the resurrection of Christ from the dead?
2	Is it reasonable to believe that Jesus rose from the dead?
3	What evidence exists that Jesus rose from the dead?
4	What do I believe is reasonable about the resurrection?
5	Can I articulate a clear apologetic for the resurrection of Christ from the dead?
Unit 8	Returning: Will Jesus return?
1	How does the life of Christ fit into the eternal plan of God?
2	Where is Jesus now?
3	How does the return of Christ fit into the eternal plan of God?
4	What will He do when He returns?
5	How should my beliefs influence my current life?
Unit 9	Response: Who do I say that He is?
1	What is the meaning of worship?
2	What functional saviors compete for prominence in my life?
3	What will be my response to the invitation of Christ?
4	How will I articulate what I have learned?

7

Course Overview

Gospel Project
Gospel check due dates

Gospel check 1
John 1–2   Due _____

Gospel check 2
John 3–8   Due _____

Gospel check 3
John 9–15   Due _____

Gospel check 4
John 16–21   Due _____

Gospel check 5
Matthew 1–7   Due _____

Gospel check 6
Matthew 8–14   Due _____

Gospel check 7
Matthew 15–21   Due _____

Gospel check 8
Matthew 22–28   Due _____

Gospel check 9
Luke 1–7   Due _____

Gospel check 10
Luke 8–14   Due _____

Gospel check 11
Luke 15–21   Due _____

Gospel check 12
Luke 22–24   Due _____

Gospel check 13
Mark 1–7   Due _____

Final project
Mark 8–16   Due _____

WHEATON PRESS
READ. RESPOND. REFLECT.

JESUS

They went to **Capernaum**, and when the Sabbath came, Jesus went into the **synagogue** and began to teach. The people were amazed at his teaching, because he taught them as one who had authority, not as the teachers of the law. Just then a man in their synagogue who was possessed by an impure spirit cried out, *"What do you want with us, Jesus of Nazareth?"*

Mark 1:21-24a

Unit Essential Questions

1   What is the desired outcome of this class?

2   What can I expect during and after this class?

Unit Learning Objectives

A   To understand the essential questions, learning objectives, and expectations this class

B   To identify my personal learning needs

C   To develop a personalized learning plan for this class

D   To understand the significance of this class and the course assignments in the overall scheme of life

Unit Learning Assessments

Expectations for growth personal reflection handout

The global student assessment

Final exam pre–assessment

Personal spiritual formation assessment

Daily Essential Questions

1   What is the learning goal for this workbook, *Life of Christ*?

2   What do I currently know about Jesus?

3   What is the Gospel Project?

4   What is the context for the essential question for this class?

5   What does John 1–2 reveal about Christ?

6   How does our culture view Christ?

My Expectations

1 The name that I like to be called is (nickname) _____.

2 The reason that I'm taking this class is because (other than because it's required):

3 One thing that I'm looking forward to in this class is:

4 Two things that I want to learn in this class include:

1)

2)

5 One goal that I have for myself this year is:

6 One thing that my teacher could pray for me about this semester would be:

7 My relationship with Jesus up this point in my life could best be described as:

My Best Class Ever

Part I. Individual Response

What was the best class that I have ever been a part of?

What made it the best class ever?

What did the teacher do to make it the best class ever?

What did I do to make it the best class ever?

What did the other students in the class do to make it the best class ever?

Part II. Pair and Share

Three ideas I really liked that I heard from someone else include:

One thing I think we should commit to, as a class, to make this the best class ever is:

Name: _____ Period: _____

1. What are the three primary offices that are woven through the Old Testament and fulfilled in Jesus Christ?

    1.

    2.

    3.

2. Who does Paul claim was the greatest Old Testament prophet?

3. How many synoptic Gospels are in the orthodox New Testament canon?

4. How much of the Bible was prophetic at the time of its original writing?

5. Over how long of a period of time was the Old Testament written?

6. How would you explain to a friend the prophecies about Christ in the Old Testament that have yet to be fulfilled?

7. When can we expect the remaining Old and New Testament prophecies about Christ to be fulfilled?

8. Explain in your own words: Why does it matter if Jesus was or was not fully divine?

9. How would a lack of full divinity affect Christ's roles from the tri–perspective view of Christ? Explain the implications for each role specifically:

-

-

-

10. At what point in His life and ministry did Jesus become fully divine?

11. What Old Testament name is the name Jesus is derived from?

12. What does the name Jesus mean?

13. Roughly how many years ago was Jesus born?

14. What does the title Christ mean?

List a few specific core beliefs about the nature and person of Christ for the following cults or religious movements:

15. Emergent Christians:

16. Jehovah's Witnesses:

17. Mormonism:

18. Unitarian Universalism:

19. Scientology:

20. Buddhism:

21. Islam:

22. Followers of Mahatma Gandhi:

23. When Jesus refers to himself as the "Son of Man," what is it a reference to?

24. You are sitting at a coffee shop with a friend. During the discussion he says, "Jesus never claimed to be God, so why would you believe that he is?" What is your response?

    A. Is your friend's statement true? Why or why not?

    B. If you claim that your friend's statement is false, where would you go in Scripture to show what you believe? (explain your response)

25. With regard to the claims of Jesus, C.S. Lewis wrote that Jesus could only be one of three things. Lewis concluded that the third was Lord. What are the first two?

    •

    •

26. Define the word incarnation.

27. Some groups who professed heresies concerning the person of Christ include the Ebionites, Gnostics, Arians, and Apollinarians. Explain how each heresy views Christ:

28. Explain why the Gnostic and Arian view of Jesus is not compatible with Scripture:

29. What New Testament book was written in large part to defend that Jesus was fully human, with a real physical body?

30. If Jesus had not been fully human, what aspect of the tri–perspective view of Christ would be null and void?

31. What vital doctrine of orthodox faith regarding the person of Christ was discussed, debated, and ratified during the Council of Chalcedon?

32. Define the Greek word hypostasis and explain why it is significant.

33. Define the Greek word kenosis and explain why it is significant.

34. Define the term Hypostatic Union and explain why it is significant.

35. Where in Scripture is the key passage that describes the kenosis found?

Define the following words from a theological perspective:

36. Propitiation:

37. Expiation:

38. Atonement:

39. Penal Substitutionary Atonement:

40. Substitution:

41. Imputation:

42. Justification:

43. Sanctification:

44. Glorification:

45. Forbearance:

46. Scapegoat:

47. Day of Atonement:

48. Reconciliation:

49. List three ways the Apostle Paul uses the word saved in the New Testament. Give Scripture references to support your answers.

    A.

    B.

    C.

50. List three ways that Christ's death fulfilled the Old Testament sacrificial system. Give Scripture references to support your answers.

    A.

    B.

    C.

51. Did Jesus have to die? Why or why not? Explain your answer with Scripture.

52. How is both the perfect love and perfect wrath of God displayed through the cross of Christ?

53. What term was created to describe the amount of pain an individual experienced during the process of crucifixion? What does the word literally mean?

53. Give three historical pieces of evidence that Jesus rose from the dead.

    A.

    B.

    C.

55. Give three non–biblical/circumstantial pieces of evidence that Jesus rose from the dead.

    A.

    B.

    C.

56. Give three biblical references that state that Jesus rose from the dead.

    A.

    B.

    C.

57. Where is Jesus today? Defend your answer using Scripture.

Reflection

What are my initial thoughts and impressions after taking the pre–assessment?

Questions for discussion and consideration:

1. What do I already know, and what do I need to learn?

2. How do I grow to reflect Christ in every area of my life if I don't know who He is?

3. How do I equip others to grow to reflect Christ if I don't know who He is?

Reflection

What is the Gospel Project?

"Take the helmet of salvation and the sword of the Spirit, which is the word of God."

Ephesians 6:17

"For the word of God is alive and active. Sharper than any double–edged sword, it penetrates even to dividing soul and spirit, joints and marrow; it judges the thoughts and attitudes of the heart."

Hebrews 4:12

How to get the most out of the Gospel Project

"Your word is a lamp unto my feet, and a light unto my path." Psalm 119:104-105

Why read the Bible?

Imagine being in a room with absolutely no light. You are surrounded by total darkness. No map. No one to hold your hand. No sense of direction and no idea if even just one step in any direction will contain safety or if it will plunge you into even more pain. What feelings or emotions would you experience? How confident would you be? What would be your response?

When even a single beam light is introduced into that type of environment, the entire situation is transformed. Now, instead of darkness, there is light. Instead of confusion, you can see the paths of safety as well as the ways that would lead you to pain or destruction. Instead of feelings of fear, you could enjoy the confidence that accompanies feelings of security.

Light changes everything

God tells us that His word, as revealed and recorded in the Bible, can transform us. It has the opportunity to be a lamp to our feet and a light to our path.

But too often we approach our journey through life lost in the darkness of our thoughts, opinions, or even in our hopes about what the Bible might say rather than being students of God's Word and walking in obedience with the confidence of what it means.

To move from fear to confidence, we must intentionally become students who carry the Word of God in our hearts and not just in our technological devices.

We need to become students of God's Word who are not swayed by the fears or opinions of others, but who exhibit the character of the wise man who built his house on the solid rock of understanding and obedience to the Word of God.

As you begin this project, ask God to give you a hunger and a thirst for His Word.

Examine™

CHRIST-CENTERED FORMATION RESOURCE

"Everyone ought to examine themselves before
they eat of the bread and drink from the cup."

1 Corinthians 11:28, NLT

Wheaton Press
Train. Equip. Reflect.

25

Where are you?
Read. Respond. Reflect.

Directions: Read through the verses below and highlight or underline any words or phrases that seem to reflect or resonate with where you are at.

Skeptic. Presented with the person of Christ and the Gospel multiple times, I demonstrate disinterest or unbelief.

"Even after Jesus had performed so many signs in their presence, they still would not believe in him." John 12:37, NIV

Characteristics: Calloused heart, dull ears, closed eyes.

"[F]or this people's heart has grown callous, their ears are dull of hearing, they have closed their eyes." Mt 13:15a, WEB

Christ's Next-Step Invitation: Repent. Believe.

"Then he began to denounce the cities in which most of his mighty works had been done, because they didn't repent." Matthew 11:20 , WEB

Growth Barrier: A lack of spiritual understanding.

"When anyone hears the message about the kingdom and does not understand it, the evil one comes and snatches away what was sown in their heart. This is the seed sown along the path." Matthew 13:19, NIV

Spiritual Need: A loving and praying friend, a change of mind and heart initiated by the Holy Spirit.

"He said to them, 'This kind can come out by nothing, except by prayer and fasting.'" Mark 9:29, WEB

"As for you, you were dead in your transgressions and sins, in which you used to live when you followed the ways of this world and of the ruler of the kingdom of the air, the spirit who is now at work in those who are disobedient." Ephesians 2:1-2, NIV

Seeker. Questioning, with a desire to learn more about Jesus.

"He answered, 'And who is he, sir? Tell me, so that I may believe in him.'" John 9:36, ISV

Characteristics: A ready heart, open ears, questions with an interest to learn more about Jesus.

"Again, the next day, John was standing with two of his disciples, and he looked at Jesus as he walked, and said, 'Behold, the Lamb of God!' The two disciples heard him speak, and they followed Jesus. Jesus turned, and saw them following, and said to them, 'What are you looking for?' They said to him, 'Rabbi' (which is to say, being interpreted, Teacher), 'where are you staying?' He said to them, 'Come, and see.' They came and saw where he was staying, and they stayed with him that day. It was about the tenth hour." John 1:35-39, WEB

Christ's Next-Step Invitation: Repent. Believe.

"Now after John was taken into custody, Jesus came into Galilee, preaching the Good News of God's Kingdom, and saying, 'The time is fulfilled, and God's Kingdom is at hand! Repent, and believe in the Good News.'" Mark 1:14-15, WEB

Growth Barrier: A lack of clear presentation and understanding of the Gospel, a lack of invitation.

"How, then, can people call on someone they have not believed? And how can they believe in someone they have not heard about? And how can they hear without someone preaching?" Romans 10:14, ISV

Spiritual Need: A clear gospel presentation and an invitation to believe and receive salvation.

"But to all who did receive him, who believed in his name, he gave the right to become children of God." John 1:12, ESV

Believer. Presented with the Gospel I believe.

"He said, 'Lord, I believe!' and he worshiped him." John 9:38 WEB

Characteristics: Seed begins to germinate, shallow soil, little or no roots.

"Other seeds fell on rocky ground, where they did not have much soil, and immediately they sprang up, since they had no depth of soil, but when the sun rose they were scorched. And since they had no root, they withered away." Matthew 13:5-6

Christ's Next Step Invitation: Follow.

"And he said to them, 'Follow me, and I will make you fishers of men.'" Matthew 4:19, ESV

Growth Barrier: Lack of roots, lack of knowledge, testing, trouble, persecution.

"These in the same way are those who are sown on the rocky places, who, when they have heard the word, immediately receive it with joy. They have no root in themselves, but are short-lived. When oppression or persecution arises because of the word, immediately they stumble." Mark 4:16-17, WEB

Spiritual Need: Prayer, roots, knowledge, biblical teaching, time, worship and someone to walk with them.

"Like newborn infants, long for the pure spiritual milk, that by it you may grow up into salvation." 1 Peter 2:2, ESV

"So then, just as you received Christ Jesus as Lord, continue to live your lives in him, rooted and built up in him, strengthened in the faith as you were taught, and overflowing with thankfulness." Colossians 2:6-7, NIV

"We continually ask God to fill you with the knowledge of His will through all the wisdom and understanding that the Spirit gives, so that you may live a life worthy of the Lord and please Him in every way: bearing fruit in every good work, growing in the knowledge of God, being strengthened with all power according to His glorious might so that you may have great endurance and patience, and giving joyful thanks to the Father, who has qualified you to share in the inheritance of His holy people in the kingdom of light." Colossians 1:9-12, NIV

Follower. Growing in faith and love; deepening roots and knowledge; struggling with thorns, trials, forgiveness, doubt, and perseverance.

"By this all people will know that you are my disciples, if you have love for one another." John 13:35, ESV

Characteristics: Beginning to push through the soil, struggling with thorns and weeds.

"Others fell among thorns. The thorns grew up and choked them." Matthew 13:7, WEB

"And calling the crowd to him with his disciples, he said to them, 'If anyone would come after me, let him deny himself and take up his cross and follow me.'" Mark 8:34, ESV

Christ's Next-Step Invitation: Deny self; pick up cross; trust, obey, and love Christ and others.

"Then Jesus said to his disciples, 'If anyone desires to come after me, let him deny himself, and take up his cross, and follow me.'" Matthew 16:24, WEB

Growth Barrier: Thorns, worries of this life, doubt, deceitfulness of wealth, comfort, self and self-will.

"Others are those who are sown among the thorns. These are those who have heard the word, and the cares of this age, and the deceitfulness of riches, and the lusts of other things entering in choke the word, and it becomes unfruitful." Mark 4:18-19,

Spiritual Need: Deny self; trials; endurance, perseverance, time, small group relationships, and accountability.

"Consider it pure joy, my brothers and sisters, whenever you face trials of many kinds, because you know that the testing of your faith produces perseverance. Let perseverance finish its work so that you may be mature and complete, not lacking anything." James 1:2-4, NIV

"Through him we have also obtained access by faith into this grace in which we stand, and we rejoice in hope of the glory of God. Not only that, but we rejoice in our sufferings, knowing that suffering produces endurance, and endurance produces character, and character produces hope." Romans 5:2-4, ESV

"These have come so that the proven genuineness of your faith—of greater worth than gold, which perishes even though refined by fire—may result in praise, glory and honor when Jesus Christ is revealed." 1 Peter 1:7, NIV

Friend. Marked by obedient love for Christ and others; may wrestle with isolation, complacency and accountability.

"You are my friends if you do what I command you." John 15:14, ESV

Characteristics: Good soil, obedience to Christ, fruit, growing faith, increasing love and perseverance in trials.

"We ought always to thank God for you, brothers and sisters, and rightly so, because your faith is growing more and more, and the love all of you have for one another is increasing. Therefore, among God's churches we boast about your perseverance and faith in all the persecutions and trials you are enduring." 2 Thessalonians 1:3-4, NIV

Christ's Next-Step Invitation: Love, obey, go, teach.

"If you love me, you will keep my commandments." John 14:15, ESV

"Jesus came to them and spoke to them, saying, 'All authority has been given to me in heaven and on earth. Go, and make disciples of all nations, baptizing them in the name of the Father and of the Son and of the Holy Spirit, teaching them to observe all things that I commanded you. Behold, I am with you always, even to the end of the age.' Amen." Mt 28:18-20,

Growth Barrier: Complacency, fear, pride, lack of vision, and lack of equipping.

"Then he said to his disciples, 'The harvest indeed is plentiful, but the laborers are few.'" Matthew 9:37, WEB

"How, then, can people call on someone they have not believed? And how can they believe in someone they have not heard about? And how can they hear without someone preaching?" Romans 10:14, ISV

Spiritual Need: Vision, continued obedience, equipping, empowerment, continued spurring and accountability within community.

" … to equip his people for works of service, so that the body of Christ may be built up until we all reach unity in the faith and in the knowledge of the Son of God and become mature, attaining to the whole measure of the fullness of Christ." Ephesians 4:12-13, NIV

"As for you, brothers, do not grow weary in doing good." 2 Thessalonians 3:13, ESV

"Let us continue to hold firmly to the hope that we confess without wavering, for the one who made the promise is faithful. And let us continue to consider how to motivate one another to love and good deeds, not neglecting to meet together, as is the habit of some, but encouraging one another even more as you see the day of the Lord coming nearer." Hebrews 10:23-25, ISV

Fisherman. Reflecting Christ and reproducing fruit of righteousness and good works.

"Because we have heard of your faith in Christ Jesus and of the love you have for all God's people—the faith and love that spring from the hope stored up for you in heaven and about which you have already heard in the true message of the gospel that has come to you. In the same way, the gospel is bearing fruit and growing throughout the whole world—just as it has been doing among you since the day you heard it and truly understood God's grace." Colossians 1:4-6, NIV

Characteristics: Good soil, fruitfulness, harvest, influence, reflecting Christ.

"Others fell on good soil, and yielded fruit: some one hundred times as much, some sixty, and some thirty." Mt 13:8, WEB

Christ's Next-Step Invitation: Teach others.

"Therefore, as you go, disciple people in all nations, baptizing them in the name of the Father, and the Son, and the Holy Spirit, teaching them to obey everything that I've commanded you." Matthew 28:19-20a, ISV

Growth Barrier: Complacency, fear, pride, lack of vision, lack of equipping, weariness.

"Let's not get tired of doing what is good, for at the right time we will reap a harvest—if we do not give up." Galatians 6:9, ISV

"Think about the one who endured such hostility from sinners, so that you may not become tired and give up." Heb 12:3,

Spiritual Need: Perseverance, humility, faithfulness, accountability, reliable people.

"It gave me great joy when some believers came and testified about your faithfulness to the truth, telling how you continue to walk in it." 3 John 3, NIV

"And what you have heard from me in the presence of many witnesses entrust to faithful men who will be able to teach others also." 2 Timothy 2:2, ESV

Examine™ Spiritual Formation Planning Tool

More resources available at WheatonPress.com

Directions: Answer the following seven questions using the words or phrases you highlighted or underlined.

1. Where am I?
Skeptic. When presented with the Gospel, I do not believe.
Seeker. Questioning, with a desire to learn more about Jesus.
Believer. Presented with the Gospel, I chose to believe.
Follower. Growing in faith, love, and roots. Struggling with thorns, trials, and perseverance.
Friend. Marked by obedient love for Christ and others.
Fisherman. Reflecting Christ and bearing fruit of righteousness and good works.

2. Where would I like to be in six months?
Skeptic. When presented with the Gospel, I do not believe.
Seeker. Questioning, with a desire to learn more about Jesus.
Believer. Presented with the Gospel, I chose to believe.
Follower. Growing in faith, love, and roots. Struggling with thorns, trials, and perseverance.
Friend. Marked by obedient love for Christ and others.
Fisherman. Reflecting Christ and bearing fruit of righteousness and good works.

3. What invitation do I need to respond to in order to take my next step?
Skeptic. Repent.
Seeker. Repent. Believe.
Believer. Follow.
Follower. Deny self. Pick up cross. Obey. Love Christ and others.
Friend. Love. Obey. Go.
Fisherman. Teach others.

4. What barriers will I face?
Skeptic. Calloused heart, deaf ears, closed eyes.
Seeker. Lack of clear testimony. Lack of invitation.
Believer. Lack of root. Testing. Trouble. Persecution.
Follower. Thorns. Worries of this life. Deceitfulness of wealth. Comfort. Self.
Friend. Complacency. Fear. Lack of vision. Lack of equipping.
Fisherman. Complacency. Fear. Lack of vision. Lack of equipping. Weariness.

5. What spiritual needs do I have?
Skeptic. Prayer. Repentance. A believing friend.
Seeker. Receive. Believe. Salvation.
Believer. Prayer. Roots. Knowledge. Teaching. Worship. Time.
Follower. Deny self. Trials. Endurance. Perseverance. Time. Small group relationships and
    accountability.
Friend. Vision. Continued obedience. Equipping. Opportunity. Empowerment. Accountability within
    community.
Fisherman. Perseverance. Faithfulness. Reliable people.

6. What steps will I take?

7. Who will I ask to hold me accountable?

Christ and Culture Artifact
Interviews and Dialogue

Part I. Interviews

Directions:

Conduct a brief, two-question interview with three different people. Your assignment is simply to ask the following questions, listen, and record their answers:

1. How is Christ portrayed in our culture?

2. How has culture changed your perspective of Christ over the course of your life?

You will submit a paragraph summary for each of the three interviews that you conduct (three paragraphs total for the interview section).

Your fourth, final paragraph will be a brief description of your artifact (see part II below). Explain why you chose it and how it represents how culture portrays Christ.

**NOTE:
- At least one person needs to be a family member, and at least one person needs to be a student who is not participating in this class (and preferably who is not a student at this school).
- This assignment would make a great "meal-time" discussion with your family.

Part II. Artifact

Directions:

Identify an artifact of how Christ is portrayed in our culture and bring it into class to share.

Part III. Class Discussion

Class Dialogue and Reflection

1. Based on our initial assessments, what do we currently know, and what do we need to learn?

2. How is Christ being presented by our current culture?

3. How does culture influence our perspective of Christ?

4. How is our perspective of Christ currently influencing culture?

What does it mean to hagah (meditate)?
Word Study

Notes and Discussion

What does it mean to halak?
Passage Study: Mark 8

Notes and Discussion

How to get the most out of the Gospel Project

"Your word is a lamp unto my feet, and a light unto my path."
Psalm 119:104-105

Ten simple steps to getting the most out of your time with God.

1. Schedule a regular time.

Make it a priority to spend time with God.

To make investing time with God each day a priority, we need to decide ahead of time to schedule our time with God. This means that before "things getting busy" or the day merely passes us by, we need to make a date with God.

Schedule a consistent time to spend with Him each day. Make it a priority. Get out a calendar or your day timer and schedule your time with God in advance.

I will spend time with God at

_____

2. Begin with the right motivation.

Our goal is not to read God's Word as merely a means to complete a project or an assignment any more than it is to be better informed moral platitudes or ways to improve our level of comfort in life. Our goal should be to gain a clearer picture of who   God is, who we are, and how we are to live out our purpose of reflecting Him.

Our motivation should be love.

First, approach your time in God's Word out of a motivation of love, not out of obligation.

> The Bible says that we love Him because He first loved us.
> 1 John 4:19

> The Bible also tells us that a love for Christ should be what compels us and motivates our lives.
> 2 Corinthians 5:14

If you don't "feel" a *love* toward God's Word, consider the invitation given by Jesus that we do not have because we have not asked.
> John 14:13-14

Have you taken a moment and asked God to place love for His Word in your heart?
> James 4:3

Second, approach your reading and reflecting on God's Word like you would approach a relationship with a friend or a loved one that you desire to get to know.

The Bible is God's way of revealing Himself to us so that we can understand and live in His design for our lives to become more evident reflections of His image within our generation.
> Ephesians 5:1-2

3. Invite the Spirit of God to lead and guide you.

Begin each time with God with a simple prayer from Psalm 119:18, asking God to open your eyes and reveal His truths to you during your time. "Open my eyes to see the wonderful truths in your instructions."

For who knows a person's thoughts except for the spirit of that person, which is in him? So also no one comprehends the thoughts of God except the Spirit of God.
> 1 Corinthians 2:10-11

Begin each time you sit down to read God's Word by inviting the Holy Spirit to share   His thoughts with you. After all, it was The Spirit of God who authored the Bible in the first place. Who better to request understanding from than the author?
> 2 Timothy 3:16

Ten simple steps to getting the most out of your time with God.

4. Commit to studying the text and not merely reading it.

Make it goal to read each set of verses several times and in various ways.

Some suggestions include:

- reading silently;

- reading aloud;

- reading a whole passage (or even book) without stopping;

- reading the verses in different translations;

- reading back to God as a prayer.

Read the Bible and use the study prompts, but do not be afraid to use online resources including translations, lexicons, and reliable commentaries to help equip you in the process of learning to understand and apply God's Word.

There is a list of helpful websites and resources on the resource page at the back of this unit.

5. Next, study and examine the text by asking, "What does it say?"

After reading the passage, go back through and write out any main ideas.

- What happened in the passage?

- Use the words directly from the text without paraphrasing the thoughts.

First, write out any questions that you may have about the passage or any initial thoughts or impressions from your first reading of it.

Use the TOPS questions to begin to dig deeper into what you are reading and what God is showing you.

- Truth – is there a Truth to apply?
- Obey – is there a command to Obey?
- Promise – is there a Promise to claim?
- Sin – is there a Sin for me to confess?

Read through the passage once and then use the notes section on the left side of the journal to begin jotting down some initial thoughts.

For example, start by identifying the context of the passage.

Is that particular chapter merely a recording of a specific historical event, or is it intended to give us an explicit instruction or direction about what to believe or how to behave?

Determining the context will help you determine the application.

Next, write out any specifics that seem important or relevant. Was there a word or a concept that was repeated or a phrase that sounded familiar?

Jot those down or highlight them in your Bible. Perhaps those words would make a new word or concept study.

Next, look for a precept, a principle, or how the person of Christ is revealed.

Ten simple steps to getting the most out of your time with God.

Look to see if there is an instruction, command, or precept from God that you need to apply and obey.

Does God reveal a promise of protection or a promised provision that is attached to a principle designed for us to understand and embrace?

How or what does the passage reveal to us about the person of Jesus Christ?

Write down any questions you have or things that don't make sense.

6. Ask, "What does this mean?"

What is God showing you in this passage?

Is He encouraging you, equipping you, or advising you?

7. Ask God to show you an application:

Do not merely listen to the word, and so deceive yourselves. Do what it says.

James 1:2

Approach your application with the understanding that the application of God's Word to our life is not for behavior modification or as an attempt to earn His favor or receive a blessing.

Applying God's Word to our life is not about achieving our own "works of righteousness." It is about reflecting the perfect righteousness of Christ through our lives.

Titus 3:5

With this perspective, we should approach God's Word with a sense of humility as we grow in our love and desire to reflect Him more with our lives.

Philippians 2:5-11

Note: It is essential to recognize that not every passage will have a noticeable or immediate application.

Your job is not to create something where it does not exist. It is merely to be obedient during the times when God does reveal something specific.

Don't be surprised if you find the application difficult. It is.

To prayerfully meditate over a passage and not just scan it for information takes work.

Satan is real. Increasing your level of information is not a threat to Satan as much as applying God's truth to your life, and experiencing transformation is a danger to him.

Asking God to show you how to apply a particular passage or set of verses to your life is the transformational part of growing in your relationship with Jesus.

In addition to being hard work and experiencing resistance from Satan, don't be surprised to find yourself resisting application too.

Change is something that we naturally tend to resist in our lives. It's essential to commit to the hard work of application.

Avoiding distractions during this part of your study is crucial. Ask God to transform you with His truth; it's a prayer that He loves to answer.

Ten simple steps to getting the most out of your time with God.

Write out your application. Make it personal and make it SMART.

Personalize it: "As a result of this passage, … "

The best application is a SMART application.

SPECIFIC: Is my application-specific?

Rather than merely saying, "I need to pray more," make a specific application. "For the next two weeks, I will pray 5 minutes a day that my three unsaved friends would come to know and believe in Jesus as their Savior."

MEASURABLE: Is my application measurable?

Instead of writing, "I need to pray more," make it measurable. "I will invest 5 minutes a day praying these five specific verses for each member of my family."

APPLICATIONAL: How does my application impact my life?

- Make sure that you write your statement in a transformational way.

- Ask yourself the question, "What difference will this make?"

REALISTIC: Is my application practical?

The reality is that you won't be able to "read through the whole Bible by the end of the week," or "pray 4 hours a day" next week.

But you may want to make it a goal that you increase your time with God to 30 minutes a day for the next 30 days. Make sure that your goal stretches you, but that it is also realistic.

TIME BOUND: When will I accomplish this goal?

Put a measurable amount of time on your application. For example, "By tomorrow night, I will write a note to my friend and apologize to them for the hurt that I caused."

8. Consider the invitations of Christ in your approach to God's application for you.

Use the invitations of Christ as an outline to help you understand the passage itself by asking what Jesus is inviting you to respond to through the passage.

- **Repent** – Is there an attitude or action God is using His Word to invite us to change?

- **Believe** – Is there a pattern of thought or false beliefs that God is revealing to us that needs to change?

- **Follow** – Is there a specific next step or area of our life that Jesus is inviting us to imitate Him?

- **Love and Deny** – Is there an area of our life where God is asking us to trust Him?

- **Go and Teach** – Is God confirming something He is doing in or through our life?

  Is He inviting us to boldly step out and share what He has taught us with someone else?

9. Set your heart and meditate on the Word of God for encouragement and inspiration.

> **Practical tip:** Keep some index cards near your journal, and when you find a particular verse that you need to be reminded of, write the verse down on the card and take it with you.

Ten simple steps to getting the most out of your time with God.

10. Read. Respond. Reflect.

READ

- Open your time in prayer and invite the Holy Spirit to guide you as you read.
- Then read the passage of Scripture several times.
- Read the passage and write out what you see.
- Circle, underline, or mark the text to help you pick out keywords or concepts that will help you in your study.
- Begin with the first verse and make a list of the most obvious facts.
- List the precepts. If you find a precept, don't paraphrase when you write it out. Instead use the literal words from the text and list out what it says.
- Identify a principle, lesson, or spiritual truth from each of the facts you wrote down.

RESPOND

- Ask questions: who, what, where, when, why, how.
- Write out the TOPS Truths from the passage.

  Truth – Is there a truth to apply?
  Obey – Is there a command to obey?
  Promise – Is there a promise to claim?
  Sin – Is there a sin for me to confess?

- Reword the principles, lessons, or truths that you wrote down in the previous step in the form of personalized questions or statements.

- Write out your application using the SMART model.
  Specific,
  Measurable,
  Application,
  Realistic,
  Time-Bound

REFLECT

- What was God saying to you during your time with Him?

- How did He use that passage in the days or weeks after you read it?

- What was He instructing you to do?

- What did you need to start doing?

  Did you?

- What did you need to stop doing?

  Did you?

REFLECT

- What did you need to confess and repent of?
- How have you applied God's Word to your life?
- Are there any specific verses in this passage that you can formulate into prayers?
- If so, do that now. If not, choose one area of what you studied and close your time in prayer.

Take time to write out your prayer in either the RESPOND or REFLECT section.

Free Resources

Dr. Constables Notes

One of the best free Bible commentaries available online is called Dr. Constables Notes. Go to any search engine and put in the words, "Dr. Constables Notes," and you will immediately have access to a verse-by-verse commentary for the majority of Scripture.

Matthew Henry

Another free and helpful commentary is one that was written by Matthew Henry. Henry was a Puritan who wrote a verse-by-verse commentary of the Bible. The strength is that they are relatively brief in comparison to Dr. Constable, but the weakness is that they are sometimes difficult to read because the literary style is a bit outdated.

Bible.cc

For students of the Bible, Bible.cc is the online equivalent of what used to take several bookshelves but now can fit on your phone in your pocket.

Bible.cc has reliable commentaries as well as Concordances and Greek Lexicons to examine precisely what Greek word is being used and how many other times that word appears.

These tools take a few minutes to be introduced to but will soon prove priceless in your study.

"For Ezra had set his heart to study the Law of the LORD, and to do it and to teach his statutes and rules in Israel."
Ezra 7:1

"Do your best to present yourself to God as one approved, a worker who does not need to be ashamed and who correctly handles the word of truth."
2 Timothy 2:15

"I meditate on your precepts and consider your ways."
Psalm 119:15

"But whoever looks intently into the perfect law that gives freedom, and continues in it -- not forgetting what they have heard, but doing it--they will be blessed in what they do."
James 1:25

What does John 1 reveal about Christ?
Word Study: John 1

Explain and Illustrate

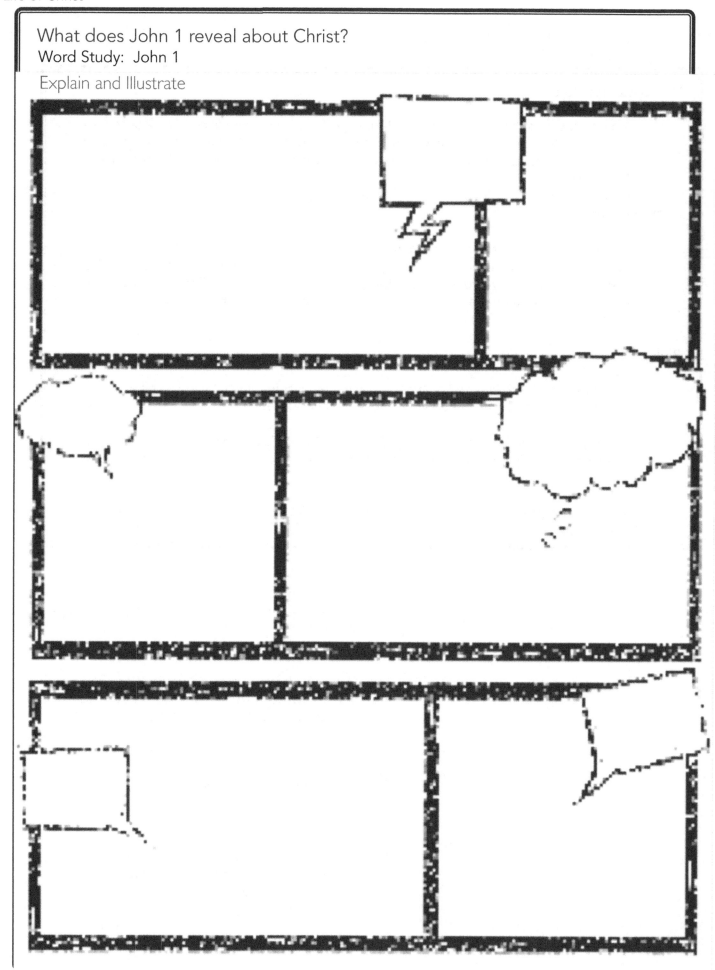

How do I understand The Allegory of the Cave?

https://commons.wikimedia.org/wiki/File:An_Illustration_of_The_Allegory_of_the_Cave,_from_Plato's_Republic.jpg

The Allegory of the Cave is a parable about a conversation between two men. One of the men is the philosopher Socrates. In the parable, Socrates describes a cave. In this cave, there are rows of people who are seated in chairs. All of the chairs and all of the people in them are sitting in a formation where they are looking at the back of the person in front of them.

Socrates describes how these individuals are chained to their chairs, and they cannot turn to the left or the right. They can only look forward. Some objects appear in front of the people. From their perspective, these objects are real. But the truth is that they are merely shadows.

What the people do not know is that behind them at the opening of the cave, there is a light. This light shines through the opening of the cave and casts shadows in front of the people sitting in the chairs.

Since the shadows are the only things that the people have ever seen, they believe that the shadows are real.

Socrates goes on to explain that one day there is a single individual who realizes that not only are the shadows in front of him not real, but the very chains that he thought kept him captive to his chair were not real either.

Upon this realization, the man stands up, turns around, and makes his way to the door of the cave. Once he steps out of the cave and into what Plato refers to as "the light," the man sees reality for the very first time.

He is so excited to discover this information that he reenters the cave to inform the others. But to his dismay, they refuse to listen or believe him and continue to sit in their chairs held by their shadowy chains and believing in a false reality.

PERSPECTIVE

Who do you say I AM?

Unit Essential Questions

1   What is the tri–perspective view of Christ?

2   How is my current perspective of Christ influencing my relationship with Jesus?

Unit Learning Objectives

A   To understand Christ's role as our prophet, priest, and king

B   To understand the various applications of the tri–perspective view of Christ on everyday life

C   To examine our life and assess our current perspective of Christ

D   To examine and understand the perspective of Christ's family on His claim to be the Messiah

Unit Learning Assessments

Tri–perspective reflection paper

Tri–perspective reflection presentation

Daily Essential Questions

1   What is the tri–perspective view of Jesus?

2   How does my perspective of Jesus influence my relationship with Him?

3   What is the application of the tri–perspective view of Christ to my life?

4   What does John 3–8 reveal about Christ?

What is the tri–perspective view of Christ?

Veronese, **The Wedding Feast at Cana** *(1563), oil on canvas. Musée du Louvre, Paris.*
The Italian artist Veronese painted the spectacular **Wedding Feast at Cana** in 1563. This massive work—measuring over 22 feet high and 32 feet long—hangs in one of the busiest galleries of the Louvre in Paris, yet despite its size and magnificence, it is often missed and/or ignored. More than 6 million visitors each year turn their backs to Veronese's masterpiece as they jostle for position and gaze through the bulletproof glass and take pictures of Leonardo da Vinci's **Mona Lisa**.

What is the application of the tri–perspective view of Christ to everyday life?

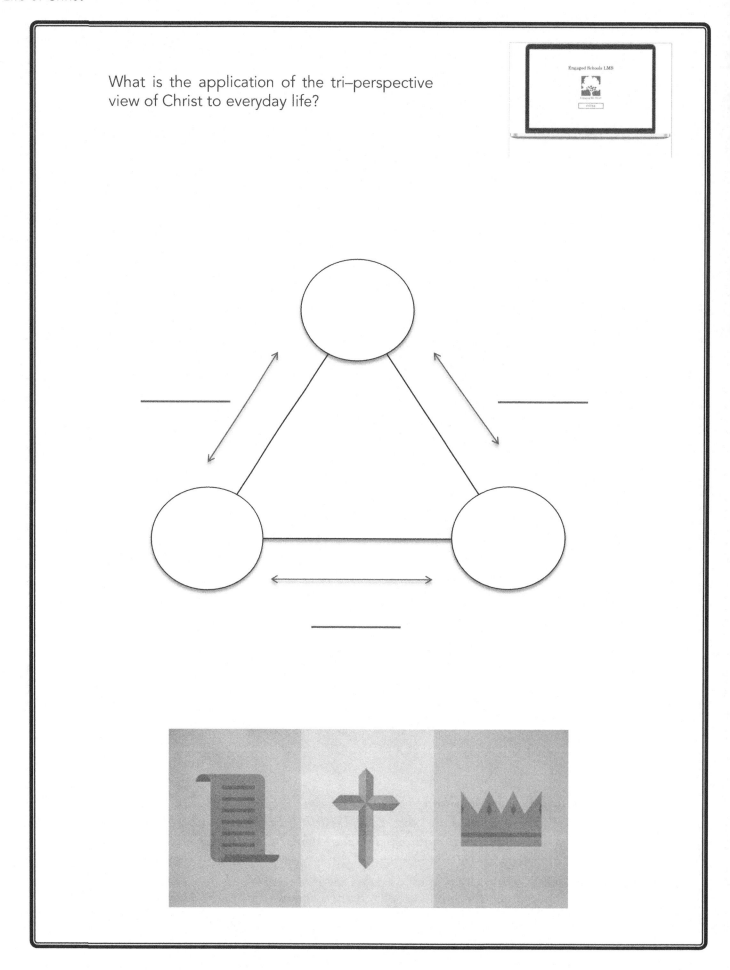

Essential Question

How is my perspective of Christ influencing my reflection of Jesus?

Learning Goal

To articulate understanding and application of the concept of the tri–perspective view of Christ

Part I. Reflection paper

Purpose: The student will use this paper to demonstrate an understanding of the concepts and application of the tri–perspective view of Christ in his or her life.

Directions: Write a 1–2 page reflection paper that demonstrates your understanding of the concepts behind the tri–perspective view of Christ and answer the four questions below, using the guidelines for a one–page paper.

- Do you most easily identify with Jesus as a prophet, priest, or king? (Demonstrate your understanding of why).
- How might this be affecting your relationship with Jesus? (Use your answer to demonstrate your understanding of the concepts involved.)
- What perspective are you lacking?
- What steps will you take to develop a fuller, more complete understanding of the person and work of Jesus?

Students will demonstrate understanding of the following concepts as articulated through the assigned reading and the classroom lectures:

The ministry of Jesus Christ as prophet, priest, and king:

A. The ministry of Jesus Christ as prophet, priest, and king
- Jesus the prophet: Ministry is to proclaim the Word of God.
     Jesus not only proclaimed the written Word of God, but was literally the incarnate, living Word of God.
- Jesus the priest: Ministry is to mediate between God and man.
     Jesus is the superior High Priest
     Jesus is the superior sacrifice
     Jesus is the superior intercessor
- Jesus the king: Ministry is to rule over all material and immaterial worlds.

B. Application of the tri–perspective view of Christ
     Religious Legalism: Jesus = Prophet + King – Priest
     Emergent Liberalism: Jesus = Priest + King – Prophet
     Evangelical Moralism: Jesus = Prophet + Priest – King

Part II. Presentation

Directions: Students will present their reflection papers in class. Presentations will be approximately 2–4 minutes long. Students will be graded on content, preparedness, attentiveness to other presenters, and how well the presentation articulates an understanding of the concepts.

Who do you say I AM?

What does John 7 reveal about Christ?

Notes and Discussion

FEAST OF
Tabernacles

Gospel Check Insights

MESSIAH

Who do you say I AM?

Mark 8:29

Is Jesus the Messiah?

Unit Essential Questions

1   Did Jesus fulfill the Old Testament prophecies from Isaiah concerning the Messiah?

2   Is Jesus the Messiah?

Unit Learning Objectives

A   To understand the connections between the Old and New Testaments regarding the Messiah

B   To examine the prophecies in the book of Isaiah regarding the Messiah

C   To examine events in the New Testament regarding the life of Christ

D   To formulate a personal apologetic regarding the reasonableness of Christ being the Messiah

Unit Learning Assessments

Prophecy project

Prophecy project reflection paper

Daily Essential Questions

1   What does the Bible tell us about the Messiah?

2   Does Jesus meet the requirements to be the Messiah?

3   How does the central theme of Scripture center on Christ?

4   What does John 9–15 reveal about Jesus?

Why does biblical prophecy matter?

Biblical prophecy is one of the ways that we can identify the Messiah.

Moses, David, Daniel, Ezekiel, Isaiah, and others prophesied about the future birth, life, death, resurrection, and return of the Messiah. Some of it would be fulfilled within the next 300 years, other parts over the period of the next 3,000. The odds of being able to "foretell" over 300 exact events concerning this single person, and then having Him fulfill each one, is nothing short of miraculous.

The Bible is full of miraculous prophecies: words spoken by humans through the inspiration of the Holy Spirit of God. In the next few class periods, you will be examining 116 specific prophecies from the book of Isaiah regarding the future Messiah.

Examine for yourself

Read Deuteronomy 18:21–22 and write in your own words what Moses says about whether or not we know if a message has been spoken by the Lord:

What does this mean? What are the implications of the words of Moses?

Old Testament Prophecies Fulfilled by Jesus Christ

Prophecy	Description	Fulfillment
1. Gen 3:15	Seed of a woman (virgin birth)	Gal 4:4-5; Matt 1:18
2. Gen 3:15	He will bruise Satan's head	Heb 2:14; 1 John 3:8
3. Gen 5:24	The bodily ascension to heaven illustrated	Mark 16:19
4. Gen 9:26-27	The God of Shem will be the Son of Shem	Luke 3:36
5. Gen 12:3	Seed of Abraham will bless all nations	Gal 3:8; Acts 3:25-26
6. Gen 12:7	The Promise made to Abraham's Seed	Gal 3:16
7. Gen 14:18	A priest after the order of Melchizedek	Heb 6:20
8. Gen 14:18	King of Peace and Righteousness	Heb 7:2
9. Gen 14:18	The Last Supper foreshadowed	Matt 26:26-29
10. Gen 17:19	Seed of Isaac (Gen 21:12)	Rom 9:7
11. Gen 22:8	The Lamb of God promised	John 1:29
12. Gen 22:18	As Isaac's seed, will bless all nations	Gal 3:16
13. Gen 26:2-5	The Seed of Isaac promised as the Redeemer	Heb 11:18
14. Gen 28:12	The Bridge to heaven	John 1:51
15. Gen 28:14	The Seed of Jacob	Luke 3:34
16. Gen 49:10	The time of His coming	Luke 2:1-7; Gal 4:4
17. Gen 49:10	The Seed of Judah	Luke 3:33
18. Gen 49:10	Called Shiloh or One Sent	John 17:3
19. Gen 49:10	Messiah to come before Judah lost identity	John 11:47-52
20. Gen 49:10	Unto Him shall the obedience of the people be	John 10:16
21. Ex 3:13-15	The Great "I AM"	John 4:26; 8:58
22. Ex 12:5	A Lamb without blemish	Heb 9:14; 1 Pet 1:19
23. Ex 12:13	The blood of the Lamb saves from wrath	Rom 5:8
24. Ex 12:21-27	Christ is our Passover	1 Cor 5:7
25. Ex 12:46	Not a bone of the Lamb to be broken	John 19:31-36
26. Ex 15:2	His exaltation predicted as Yeshua	Acts 7:55-56
27. Ex 15:11	His Character-Holiness	Luke 1:35; Acts 4:27

Prophecy	Description	Fulfillment
28. Ex 17:6	The Spiritual Rock of Israel	1 Cor 10:4
29. Ex 33:19	His Character-Merciful	Luke 1:72
30. Lev 1:2-9	His sacrifice a sweet smelling savor unto God	Eph 5:2
31. Lev 14:11	The leper cleansed-Sign to priesthood	Luke 5:12-14; Acts 6:7
32. Lev 16:15-17	Prefigures Christ's once-for-all death	Heb 9:7-14
33. Lev 16:27	Suffering outside the Camp	Matt 27:33; Heb. 13:11-12
34. Lev 17:11	The Blood-the life of the flesh	Matt 26:28; Mark 10:45
35. Lev 17:11	It is the blood that makes atonement	Rom. 3:23-24; 1 John 1:7
36. Lev 23:36-37	The Drink-offering: "If any man thirst"	John 7:37
37. Num 9:12	Not a bone of Him broken	John 19:31-36
38. Num 21:9	The serpent on a pole-Christ lifted up	John 3:14-18; 12:32
39. Num 24:17	Time: "I shall see him, but not now."	John 1:14; Gal 4:4
40. Deut 18:15	"This is of a truth that prophet"	John 6:14
41. Deut 18:15-16	"Had you believed Moses, you would believe me."	John 5:45-47
42. Deut 18:18	Sent by the Father to speak His word	John 8:28-29
43. Deut 18:19	Whoever will not hear must bear his sin	Acts 3:22-23
44. Deut 21:23	Cursed is he that hangs on a tree	Gal 3:10-13
45. Joshua 5:14-15	The Captain of our salvation	Heb 2:10
46. Ruth 4:4-10	Christ, our kinsman, has redeemed us	Eph 1:3-7
47. 1 Sam 2:35	A Faithful Priest	Heb. 2:17; 3:1-3, 6; 7:24-25
48. 1 Sam 2:10	Shall be an anointed King to the Lord	Matt 28:18; John 12:15
49. 2 Sam 7:12	David's Seed	Matt 1:1
50. 2 Sam 7:13	His Kingdom is everlasting	2 Pet 1:11
51. 2 Sam 7:14a	The Son of God	Luke 1:32; Rom 1:3-4
52. 2 Sam 7:16	David's house established forever	Luke 3:31; Rev 22:16
53. 2 Ki 2:11	The bodily ascension to heaven illustrated	Luke 24:51
54. 1 Chr 17:11	David's Seed	Matt 1:1; 9:27
55. 1 Chr 17:12-13	To reign on David's throne forever	Luke 1:32-33
56. 1 Chr 17:13	"I will be His Father, He...my Son."	Heb 1:5
57. Job 9:32-33	Mediator between man and God	1 Tim 2:5
58. Job 19:23-27	The Resurrection predicted	John 5:24-29
59. Psa 2:1-3	The enmity of kings foreordained	Acts 4:25-28
60. Psa 2:2	To own the title, Anointed (Christ)	John 1:41; Acts 2:36

Prophecy	Description	Fulfillment
61. Psa 2:6	His Character-Holiness	John 8:46; Rev 3:7
62. Psa 2:6	To own the title King	Matt 2:2
63. Psa 2:7	Declared the Beloved Son	Matt 3:17; Rom 1:4
64. Psa 2:7-8	The Crucifixion and Resurrection intimated	Acts 13:29-33
65. Psa 2:8-9	Rule the nations with a rod of iron	Rev 2:27; 12:5; 19:15
66. Psa 2:12	Life comes through faith in Him	John 20:31
67. Psa 8:2	The mouths of babes perfect His praise	Matt 21:16
68. Psa 8:5-6	His humiliation and exaltation	Heb 2:5-9
69. Psa 9:7-10	Judge the world in righteousness	Acts 17:31
70. Psa 16:10	Was not to see corruption	Acts 2:31; 13:35
71. Psa 16:9-11	Was to arise from the dead	John 20:9
72. Psa 17:15	The resurrection predicted	Luke 24:6
73. Psa 18:2-3	The horn of salvation	Luke 1:69-71
74. Psa 22:1	Forsaken because of sins of others	2 Cor 5:21
75. Psa 22:1	"My God, my God, why have You forsaken me?"	Matt 27:46
76. Psa 22:2	Darkness upon Calvary for three hours	Matt 27:45
77. Psa 22:7	They shoot out the lip and shake the head	Matt 27:39-44
78. Psa 22:8	"He trusted in God, let Him deliver Him"	Matt 27:43
79. Psa 22:9-10	Born the Savior	Luke 2:7
80. Psa 22:12-13	They seek His death	John 19:6
81. Psa 22:14	His blood poured out when they pierced His side	John 19:34
82. Psa 22:14-15	Suffered agony on Calvary	Mark 15:34-37
83. Psa 22:15	He thirsted	John 19:28
84. Psa 22:16	They pierced His hands and His feet	John 19:34-37; 20:27
85. Psa 22:17-18	Stripped Him before the stares of men	Luke 23:34-35
86. Psa 22:18	They parted His garments	John 19:23-24
87. Psa 22:20-21	He committed Himself to God	Luke 23:46
88. Psa 22:20-21	Satanic power bruising the Redeemer's heel	Heb 2:14
89. Psa 22:22	His Resurrection declared	John 20:17
90. Psa 22:27-28	He shall be the governor of the nations	Col 1:16
91. Psa 22:31	"It is finished"	John 19:30; Heb 10:10-12, 14, 18
92. Psa 23:1	"I am the Good Shepherd"	John 10:11; 1 Pet 2:25
93. Psa 24:3	His exaltation predicted	Acts 1:11; Phil 2:9

Prophecy	Description	Fulfillment
94. Psa 30:3	His resurrection predicted	Acts 2:32
95. Psa 31:5	"Into Your hands I commit my spirit"	Luke 23:46
96. Psa 31:11	His acquaintances fled from Him	Mark 14:50
97. Psa 31:13	They took counsel to put Him to death	Matt 27:1; John 11:53
98. Psa 31:14-15	"He trusted in God, let Him deliver him"	Matt 27:43
99. Psa 34:20	Not a bone of Him broken	John 19:31-36
100. Psa 35:11	False witnesses rose up against Him	Matt 26:59
101. Psa 35:19	He was hated without a cause	John 15:25
102. Psa 38:11	His friends stood afar off	Luke 23:49
103. Psa 38:12	Enemies try to entangle Him by craft	Mark 14:1; Matt 22:15
104. Psa 38:12-13	Silent before His accusers	Matt 27:12-14
105. Psa 38:20	He went about doing good	Acts 10:38
106. Psa 40:2-5	The joy of His resurrection predicted	John 20:20
107. Psa 40:6-8	His delight-the will of the Father	John 4:34; Heb 10:5-10
108. Psa 40:9	He was to preach the Righteousness in Israel	Matt 4:17
109. Psa 40:14	Confronted by adversaries in the Garden	John 18:4-6
110. Psa 41:9	Betrayed by a familiar friend	John 13:18
111. Psa 45:2	Words of Grace come from His lips	John 1:17; Luke 4:22
112. Psa 45:6	To own the title, God or Elohim	Heb 1:8
113. Psa 45:7	A special anointing by the Holy Spirit	Matt 3:16; Heb. 1:9
114. Psa 45:7-8	Called the Christ (Messiah or Anointed)	Luke 2:11
115. Psa 45:17	His name remembered forever	Eph 1:20-21; Heb. 1:8
116. Psa 55:12-14	Betrayed by a friend, not an enemy	John 13:18
117. Psa 55:15	Unrepentant death of the Betrayer	Matt 27:3-5; Acts 1:16-19
118. Psa 68:18	To give gifts to men	Eph 4:7-16
119. Psa 68:18	Ascended into Heaven	Luke 24:51
120. Psa 69:4	Hated without a cause	John 15:25
121. Psa 69:8	A stranger to own brethren	John 1:11; 7:5
122. Psa 69:9	Zealous for the Lord's House	John 2:17
123. Psa 69:14-20	Messiah's anguish of soul before crucifixion	Matt 26:36-45
124. Psa 69:20	"My soul is exceeding sorrowful"	Matt 26:38
125. Psa 69:21	Given vinegar in thirst	Matt 27:34
126. Psa 69:26	The Savior given and smitten by God	John 17:4; 18:11

Prophecy	Description	Fulfillment
127. Psa 72:10-11	Great persons were to visit Him	Matt 2:1-11
128. Psa 72:16	The corn of wheat to fall into the Ground	John 12:24-25
129. Psa 72:17	Belief on His name will produce offspring	John 1:12-13
130. Psa 72:17	All nations shall be blessed by Him	Gal 3:8
131. Psa 72:17	All nations shall call Him blessed	John 12:13; Rev 5:8-12
132. Psa 78:1-2	He would teach in parables	Matt 13:34-35
133. Psa 78:2b	To speak the Wisdom of God with authority	Matt 7:29
134. Psa 80:17	The Man of God's right hand	Mark 14:61-62
135. Psa 88	The Suffering and Reproach of Calvary	Matt 27:26-50
136. Psa 88:8	They stood afar off and watched	Luke 23:49
137. Psa 89:27	Firstborn	Col 1:15-18
138. Psa 89:27	Emmanuel to be higher than earthly kings	Luke 1:32-33
139. Psa 89:35-37	David's Seed, throne, kingdom endure forever	Luke 1:32-33
140. Psa 89:36-37	His character-Faithfulness	Rev 1:5; 19:11
141. Psa 90:2	He is from everlasting (Micah 5:2)	John 1:1
142. Psa 91:11-12	Identified as Messianic, used to tempt Christ	Luke 4:10-11
143. Psa 97:9	His exaltation predicted	Acts 1:11; Eph 1:20
144. Psa 100:5	His character-Goodness	Matt 19:16-17
145. Psa 102:1-11	The Suffering and Reproach of Calvary	John 19:16-30
146. Psa 102:25-27	Messiah is the Preexistent Son	Heb 1:10-12
147. Psa 109:25	Ridiculed	Matt 27:39
148. Psa 110:1	Son of David	Matt 22:42-43
149. Psa 110:1	To ascend to the right-hand of the Father	Mark 16:19
150. Psa 110:1	David's son called Lord	Matt 22:44-45
151. Psa 110:4	A priest after Melchizedek's order	Heb 6:20
152. Psa 112:4	His character-Compassionate, Gracious, et al	Matt 9:36
153. Psa 118:17-18	Messiah's Resurrection assured	Luke 24:5-7; 1 Cor 15:20
154. Psa 118:22-23	The rejected stone is Head of the corner	Matt 21:42-43
155. Psa 118:26a	The Blessed One presented to Israel	Matt 21:9
156. Psa 118:26b	To come while Temple standing	Matt 21:12-15
157. Psa 132:11	The Seed of David (the fruit of His Body)	Luke 1:32; Act 2:30
158. Psa 129:3	He was scourged	Matt 27:26
159. Psa 138:1-6	The supremacy of David's Seed amazes kings	Matt 2:2-6

Prophecy	Description	Fulfillment
160. Psa 147:3-6	The earthly ministry of Christ described	Luke 4:18
161. Prov 1:23	He will send the Spirit of God	John 16:7
162. Prov 8:23	Foreordained from everlasting	Rev 13:8; 1 Pet 1:19-20
163. Song 5:16	The altogether lovely One	John 1:17
164. Isa 2:3	He shall teach all nations	John 4:25
165. Isa 2:4	He shall judge among the nations	John 5:22
166. Isa 6:1	When Isaiah saw His glory	John 12:40-41
167. Isa 6:8	The One Sent by God	John 12:38-45
168. Isa 6:9-10	Parables fall on deaf ears	Matt 13:13-15
169. Isa 6:9-12	Blinded to Christ and deaf to His words	Acts 28:23-29
170. Isa 7:14	To be born of a virgin	Luke 1:35
171. Isa 7:14	To be Emmanuel-God with us	Matt 1:18-23; 1 Tim 3:16
172. Isa 8:8	Called Emmanuel	Matt 28:20
173. Isa 8:14	A stone of stumbling, a Rock of offense	1 Pet 2:8
174. Isa 9:1-2	His ministry to begin in Galilee	Matt 4:12-17
175. Isa 9:6	A child born-Humanity	Luke 1:31
176. Isa 9:6	A Son given-Deity	Luke 1:32; John 1:14; 1 Tim 3:16
177. Isa 9:6	Declared to be the Son of God with power	Rom 1:3-4
178. Isa 9:6	The Wonderful One, Peleh	Luke 4:22
179. Isa 9:6	The Counselor, Yaatz	Matt 13:54
180. Isa 9:6	The Mighty God, El Gibor	1 Cor 1:24; Titus 2:3
181. Isa 9:6	The Everlasting Father, Avi Adth	John 8:58; 10:30
182. Isa 9:6	The Prince of Peace, Sar Shalom	John 16:33
183. Isa 9:7	To establish an everlasting kingdom	Luke 1:32-33
184. Isa 9:7	His Character-Just	John 5:30
185. Isa 9:7	No end to his Government, Throne, and Peace	Luke 1:32-33
186. Isa 11:1	Called a Nazarene-the Branch	Matt 2:23
187. Isa 11:1	A rod out of Jesse-Son of Jesse	Luke 3:23-32
188. Isa 11:2	Anointed One by the Spirit	Matt 3:16-17; Acts 10:38
189. Isa 11:2	His Character-Wisdom, Knowledge, et al	Col 2:3
190. Isa 11:3	He would know their thoughts	Luke 6:8; John 2:25
191. Isa 11:4	Judge in righteousness	Acts 17:31
192. Isa 11:4	Judges with the sword of His mouth	Rev 2:16; 19:11, 15

Prophecy	Description	Fulfillment
193. Isa 11:5	Character: Righteous & Faithful	Rev 19:11
194. Isa 11:10	The Gentiles seek Him	John 12:18-21
195. Isa 12:2	Called Jesus-Yeshua	Matt 1:21
196. Isa 22:22	The One given all authority to govern	Rev 3:7
197. Isa 25:8	The Resurrection predicted	1 Cor 15:54
198. Isa 26:19	His power of Resurrection predicted	Matt 27:50-54
199. Isa 28:16	The Messiah is the precious corner stone	Acts 4:11-12
200. Isa 28:16	The Sure Foundation	1 Cor 3:11; Matt 16:18
201. Isa 29:13	He indicated hypocritical obedience to His Word	Matt 15:7-9
202. Isa 29:14	The wise are confounded by the Word	1 Cor 1:18-31
203. Isa 32:2	A Refuge-A man shall be a hiding place	Matt 23:37
204. Isa 35:4	He will come and save you	Matt 1:21
205. Isa 35:5-6	To have a ministry of miracles	Matt 11:2-6
206. Isa 40:3-4	Preceded by forerunner	John 1:23
207. Isa 40:9	"Behold your God"	John 1:36; 19:14
208. Isa 40:10	He will come to reward	Rev 22:12
209. Isa 40:11	A shepherd-compassionate life-giver	John 10:10-18
210. Isa 42:1-4	The Servant-as a faithful, patient redeemer	Matt 12:18-21
211. Isa 42:2	Meek and lowly	Matt 11:28-30
212. Isa 42:3	He brings hope for the hopeless	John 4
213. Isa 42:4	The nations shall wait on His teachings	John 12:20-26
214. Isa 42:6	The Light (salvation) of the Gentiles	Luke 2:32
215. Isa 42:1-6	His is a worldwide compassion	Matt 28:19-20
216. Isa 42:7	Blind eyes opened	John 9:25-38
217. Isa 43:11	He is the only Savior	Acts 4:12
218. Isa 44:3	He will send the Spirit of God	John 16:7-13
219. Isa 45:21-25	He is Lord and Savior	Phil 3:20; Titus 2:13
220. Isa 45:23	He will be the Judge	John 5:22; Rom 14:11
221. Isa 46:9-10	Declares things not yet done	John 13:19
222. Isa 48:12	The First and the Last	John 1:30; Rev 1:8, 17
223. Isa 48:16-17	He came as a Teacher	John 3:2
224. Isa 49:1	Called from the womb-His humanity	Matt 1:18
225. Isa 49:5	A Servant from the womb	Luke 1:31; Phil 2:7

Prophecy	Description	Fulfillment
226. Isa 49:6	He will restore Israel	Acts 3:19-21; 15:16-17
227. Isa 49:6	He is Salvation for Israel	Luke 2:29-32
228. Isa 49:6	He is the Light of the Gentiles	John 8:12; Acts 13:47
229. Isa 49:6	He is Salvation unto the ends of the earth	Acts 15:7-18
230. Isa 49:7	He is despised of the Nation	John 1:11; 8:48-49; 19:14-15
231. Isa 50:3	Heaven is clothed in black at His humiliation	Luke 23:44-45
232. Isa 50:4	He is a learned counselor for the weary	Matt 7:29; 11:28-29
233. Isa 50:5	The Servant bound willingly to obedience	Matt 26:39
234. Isa 50:6a	"I gave my back to those who struck Me"	Matt 27:26
235. Isa 50:6b	He was smitten on the cheeks	Matt 26:67
236. Isa 50:6c	He was spat upon	Matt 27:30
237. Isa 52:7	Published good tidings upon mountains	Matt 5:12; 15:29; 28:16
238. Isa 52:13	The Servant exalted	Acts 1:8-11; Eph 1:19-22; Phil 2:5-9
239. Isa 52:14	The Servant shockingly abused	Luke 18:31-34; Matt 26:67-68
240. Isa 52:15	Nations startled by message of the Servant	Luke 18:31-34; Matt 26:67-68
241. Isa 52:15	His blood shed sprinkles nations	Heb 9:13-14; Rev 1:5
242. Isa 53:1	His people would not believe Him	John 12:37-38
243. Isa 53:2	Appearance of an ordinary man	Phil 2:6-8
244. Isa 53:3a	Despised	Luke 4:28-29
245. Isa 53:3b	Rejected	Matt 27:21-23
246. Isa 53:3c	Great sorrow and grief	Matt 26:37-38; Luke 19:41; Heb 4:15
247. Isa 53:3d	Men hide from being associated with Him	Mark 14:50-52
248. Isa 53:4a	He would have a healing ministry	Matt 8:16-17
249. Isa 53:4b	Thought to be cursed by God	Matt 26:66; 27:41-43
250. Isa 53:5a	Bears penalty for mankind's iniquities	2 Cor 5:21; Heb 2:9
251. Isa 53:5b	His sacrifice provides peace between man and God	Col 1:20
252. Isa 53:5c	His sacrifice would heal man of sin	1 Pet 2:24
253. Isa 53:6a	He would be the sin-bearer for all mankind	1 John 2:2; 4:10
254. Isa 53:6b	God's will that He bear sin for all mankind	Gal 1:4
255. Isa 53:7a	Oppressed and afflicted	Matt 27:27-31
256. Isa 53:7b	Silent before his accusers	Matt 27:12-14
257. Isa 53:7c	Sacrificial lamb	John 1:29; 1 Pet 1:18-19
258. Isa 53:8a	Confined and persecuted	Matt 26:47-27:31

Prophecy	Description	Fulfillment
259. Isa 53:8b	He would be judged	John 18:13-22
260. Isa 53:8c	Killed	Matt 27:35
261. Isa 53:8d	Dies for the sins of the world	1 John 2:2
262. Isa 53:9a	Buried in a rich man's grave	Matt 27:57
263. Isa 53:9b	Innocent and had done no violence	Luke 23:41; John 18:38
264. Isa 53:9c	No deceit in his mouth	1 Pet 2:22
265. Isa 53:10a	God's will that He die for mankind	John 18:11
266. Isa 53:10b	An offering for sin	Matt 20:28; Gal 3:13
267. Isa 53:10c	Resurrected and live forever	Rom 6:9
268. Isa 53:10d	He would prosper	John 17:1-5
269. Isa 53:11a	God fully satisfied with His suffering	John 12:27
270. Isa 53:11b	God's servant would justify man	Rom 5:8-9, 18-19
271. Isa 53:11c	The sin-bearer for all mankind	Heb 9:28
272. Isa 53:12a	Exalted by God because of his sacrifice	Matt 28:18
273. Isa 53:12b	He would give up his life to save mankind	Luke 23:46
274. Isa 53:12c	Numbered with the transgressors	Mark 15:27-28
275. Isa 53:12d	Sin-bearer for all mankind	1 Pet 2:24
276. Isa 53:12e	Intercede to God in behalf of mankind	Luke 23:34; Rom 8:34
277. Isa 55:3	Resurrected by God	Acts 13:34
278. Isa 55:4a	A witness	John 18:37
279. Isa 55:4b	He is a leader and commander	Heb 2:10
280. Isa 55:5	God would glorify Him	Acts 3:13
281. Isa 59:16a	Intercessor between man and God	Matt 10:32
282. Isa 59:16b	He would come to provide salvation	John 6:40
283. Isa 59:20	He would come to Zion as their Redeemer	Luke 2:38
284. Isa 60:1-3	He would show light to the Gentiles	Acts 26:23
285. Isa 61:1a	The Spirit of God upon him	Matt 3:16-17
286. Isa 61:1b	The Messiah would preach the good news	Luke 4:16-21
287. Isa 61:1c	Provide freedom from the bondage of sin	John 8:31-36
288. Isa 61:1-2a	Proclaim a period of grace	Gal 4:4-5
289. Jer 23:5-6	Descendant of David	Luke 3:23-31
290. Jer 23:5-6	The Messiah would be both God and Man	John 13:13; 1 Tim 3:16
291. Jer 31:22	Born of a virgin	Matt 1:18-20

Prophecy	Description	Fulfillment
292. Jer 31:31	The Messiah would be the new covenant	Matt 26:28
293. Jer 33:14-15	Descendant of David	Luke 3:23-31
294. Ezek 34:23-24	Descendant of David	Matt 1:1
295. Ezek 37:24-25	Descendant of David	Luke 1:31-33
296. Dan 2:44-45	The Stone that shall break the kingdoms	Matt 21:44
297. Dan 7:13-14a	He would ascend into heaven	Acts 1:9-11
298. Dan 7:13-14b	Highly exalted	Eph 1:20-22
299. Dan 7:13-14c	His dominion would be everlasting	Luke 1:31-33
300. Dan 9:24a	To make an end to sins	Gal 1:3-5
301. Dan 9:24a	To make reconciliation for iniquity	Rom 5:10; 2 Cor 5:18-21
302. Dan 9:24b	He would be holy	Luke 1:35
303. Dan 9:25	His announcement	John 12:12-13
304. Dan 9:26a	Cut off	Matt 16:21; 21:38-39
305. Dan 9:26b	Die for the sins of the world	Heb 2:9
306. Dan 9:26c	Killed before the destruction of the temple	Matt 27:50-51
307. Dan 10:5-6	Messiah in a glorified state	Rev 1:13-16
308. Hos 11:1	He would be called out of Egypt	Matt 2:15
309. Hos 13:14	He would defeat death	1 Cor 15:55-57
310. Joel 2:32	Offer salvation to all mankind	Rom 10:9-13
311. Jonah 1:17	Death and resurrection of Christ	Matt 12:40; 16:4
312. Mic 5:2a	Born in Bethlehem	Matt 2:1-6
313. Mic 5:2b	Ruler in Israel	Luke 1:33
314. Mic 5:2c	From everlasting	John 8:58
315. Hag 2:6-9	He would visit the second Temple	Luke 2:27-32
316. Hag 2:23	Descendant of Zerubbabel	Luke 2:27-32
317. Zech 3:8	God's servant	John 17:4
318. Zech 6:12-13	Priest and King	Heb 8:1
319. Zech 9:9a	Greeted with rejoicing in Jerusalem	Matt 21:8-10
320. Zech 9:9b	Beheld as King	John 12:12-13
321. Zech 9:9c	The Messiah would be just	John 5:30
322. Zech 9:9d	The Messiah would bring salvation	Luke 19:10
323. Zech 9:9e	The Messiah would be humble	Matt 11:29
324. Zech 9:9f	Presented to Jerusalem riding on a donkey	Matt 21:6-9

Prophecy	Description	Fulfillment
325. Zech 10:4	The cornerstone	Eph 2:20
326. Zech 11:4-6a	At His coming, Israel to have unfit leaders	Matt 23:1-4
327. Zech 11:4-6b	Rejection causes God to remove His protection	Luke 19:41-44
328. Zech 11:4-6c	Rejected in favor of another king	John 19:13-15
329. Zech 11:7	Ministry to "poor," the believing remnant	Matt 9:35-36
330. Zech 11:8a	Unbelief forces Messiah to reject them	Matt 23:33
331. Zech 11:8b	Despised	Matt 27:20
332. Zech 11:9	Stops ministering to those who rejected Him	Matt 13:10-11
333. Zech 11:10-11a	Rejection causes God to remove protection	Luke 19:41-44
334. Zech 11:10-11b	The Messiah would be God	John 14:7
335. Zech 11:12-13a	Betrayed for thirty pieces of silver	Matt 26:14-15
336. Zech 11:12-13b	Rejected	Matt 26:14-15
337. Zech 11:12-13c	Thirty pieces of silver cast in the house of the Lord	Matt 27:3-5
338. Zech 11:12-13d	The Messiah would be God	John 12:45
339. Zech 12:10a	The Messiah's body would be pierced	John 19:34-37
340. Zech 12:10b	The Messiah would be both God and man	John 10:30
341. Zech 12:10c	The Messiah would be rejected	John 1:11
342. Zech 13:7a	God's will He die for mankind	John 18:11
343. Zech 13:7b	A violent death	Mark 14:27
344. Zech 13:7c	Both God and man	John 14:9
345. Zech 13:7d	Israel scattered as a result of rejecting Him	Matt 26:31-56
346. Zech 14:4	He would return to the Mt. of Olives	Acts 1:11-12
347. Mal 3:1a	Messenger to prepare the way for Messiah	Mark 1:1-8
348. Mal 3:1b	Sudden appearance at the temple	Mark 11:15-16
349. Mal 3:1c	Messenger of the new covenant	Luke 4:43
350. Mal 4:5	Forerunner in spirit of Elijah	Matt 3:1-3; 11:10-14; 17:11-13
351. Mal 4:6	Forerunner would turn many to righteousness	Luke 1:16-17

Prophecy Project Collaboration
Part I. Personal Reflection

Identify 5 matches you find most interesting or compelling.

1.

2.

3.

4.

5.

After identifying your five matches, respond to the questions below:

1. Explain the five passages you chose. Why did you choose those five, and how do they affect your perception of Christ as the Messiah?

2. What does God reveal about the Messiah through the verses highlighted in your discussion?

3. What have you learned or been challenged by through this project?

4. Explain the statement, "Jesus is central to all of Scripture."

5. How would your reading of God's Word change if Jesus became the center of everything in Scripture?

65

Is Jesus the Messiah?

Some of the prophecies about the coming Messiah:

- Compare Genesis 9:26–27 with Luke 3:35.

    Out of the three sons of Noah, the Messiah would come through …

- Read Genesis 12:2–3, 22:18.

    Out of the descendants of Shem, the Messiah would come through …

- Read Genesis 21:12.

    Out of the two sons of Abraham, the Messiah would come through …

- Read Genesis 35:10–12 and Numbers 24:17.

    Out of the twelve sons of Jacob, the Messiah would come not through Joseph but through…

- Read Genesis 49:10, Psalm 78:67–68, and Isaiah 11:1–2.

    Out of the descendants of Judah, all would be rejected except for the family of …

- Read Jeremiah 23:5.

    Out of all of the sons of Jesse, all would be passed over except for …

    - In other words, the Messiah would be the one who was the son of _____, the son of _____, the son of _____, the son of _____, the son of _____, the son of _____, the son of _____. It is as if the Bible gives us the exact address for ….

    Read Matthew 1 together out loud. Write out your reflection on what you see regarding the "address" of the Messiah in comparison with the prophecies from the Old Testament.

Essential Question

Did Jesus fulfill the Old Testament prophecies regarding the future Messiah in the book of Isaiah?

Learning Goal

To articulate understanding and application of the concept of the fullness of Christ

Part I. Prophecy project

Directions

Students will identify 5 compelling prophecies that were fulfilled by Christ and create a one–page prophecy reflection paper.

Part II. Prophecy project reflection paper

Purpose:

Students will use this paper to demonstrate an understanding of the concepts and application of Jesus as the Messiah and as the fulfillment of Old Testament prophecy.

- Students will demonstrate understanding of the concepts articulated through the assigned reading, the classroom lectures, and the classroom prophecy project.

- Students will demonstrate personal application and reflection of the concepts uncovered through the prophecy project, reading, lectures, and dialogue in class.

Directions

Write a one–page reflection paper that demonstrates your understanding of the concept of Christ as the fulfillment of Old Testament prophecy and answer the four questions below, using the guidelines for a one–page paper. Please attach your completed prophecy project (work from class) to your one–page reflection paper.

A.   Which prophecies (if any) were most compelling, convincing, and convicting for you?

B.   In what ways did this project make the Bible more reliable or authoritative for you?

C.   What could your response be to someone who claims Jesus simply manipulated His life in such a way that He would fulfill all the Old Testament prophecies?

D.   How is the central theme of Scripture centered on the revelation of Jesus?

WHEATON PRESS
READ. RESPOND. REFLECT.

DIVINE

Who do you say I AM?
Mark 8:29

Vasili Nesterenko. The Marriage Feast at Cana in Galilee. 2001
Wedding Feast In The Bible | Vasili Nesterenko. The Marriage Feast at Cana in Galilee. 2001 |

Unit Essential Questions

1. What do other religions teach about the divinity of Christ?

2. Did Jesus claim to be God?

3. Is it possible for Jesus to have been just a good man?

Unit Learning Objectives

A. Examine other religions and worldviews to learn their perspective on the divinity of Christ

B. Examine Scripture to discern if Jesus claimed to be the one and only God

C. Evaluate Jewish customs, traditions, and language to better understand the words and actions of Christ in the context of His generation and culture

D. Logically work through the process of whether or not it is possible for Christ to have simply been a good man

Unit Learning Assessments

Unit exam

Daily Essential Questions

1. Why would it matter whether or not that Jesus was fully divine?

2. What do other religions believe about the divinity of Jesus Christ?

3. Did Jesus claim to be God?

4. Why was Jesus crucified?

5. What is significant about the word Elohim?

6. What does John 16–21 reveal about Christ?

Bell Ringers

1. If Jesus is who He said He is then what difference does that make in my life?

2. Why does it matter if Jesus was fully divine?

3. How would a lack of full divinity affect Christ's roles from the tri–perspective view? What would be the implications for each role?

   - Prophet:

   - Priest:

   - King:

4. At what point did Jesus become fully divine?

   - How would you prove your answer from Scripture?

Is Jesus fully divine?
Notes and Discussion

What do other religions believe and teach about the divinity of Christ?
Notes and Discussion

- Scientology

- Jehovah's Witnesses

- Mormonism

- Unitarian Universalism

What do other religions believe and teach about the divinity of Christ?
Notes and Discussion

- Liberal and Emergent 'Christians'

- Arianism

- Buddhism

- Islam

- Hinduism

Did Jesus claim to be God?
Small Group Project

Part 1. Passage study: Mark 14:60–64

A. What is the context surrounding the passage?

B. What does Jesus say?

C. What does it mean?

D. How do people respond?

E. What does it mean?

F. What additional cross references or research do you need to do to understand the passage?

Part II. Class Notes and Discussion

Did Jesus claim to be God?
Small Group Project

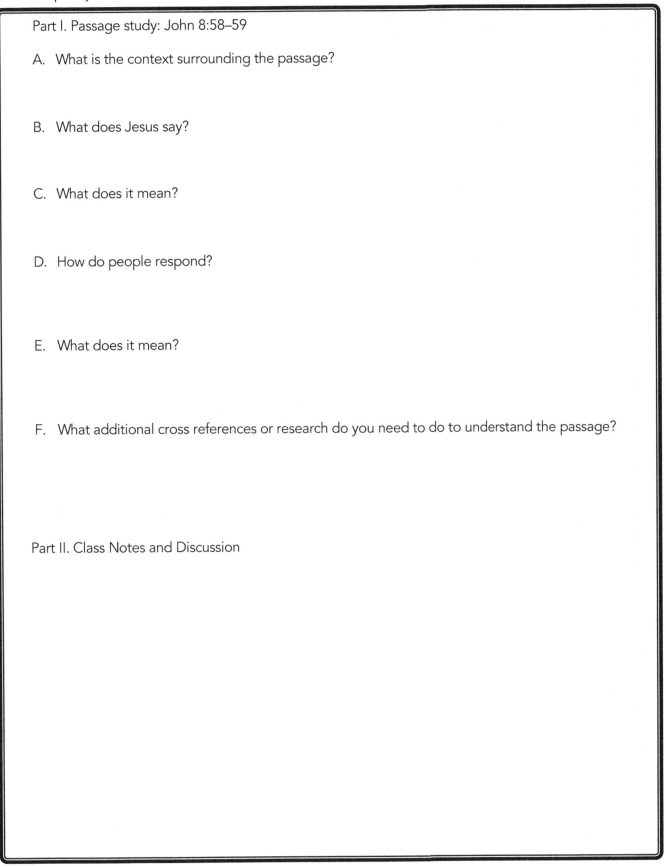

Part I. Passage study: John 8:58–59

A. What is the context surrounding the passage?

B. What does Jesus say?

C. What does it mean?

D. How do people respond?

E. What does it mean?

F. What additional cross references or research do you need to do to understand the passage?

Part II. Class Notes and Discussion

Did Jesus claim to be God?
Small Group Project

Part I. Passage study: John 10:30–31

A. What is the context surrounding the passage?

A. What does Jesus say?

B. What does it mean?

C. How do people respond?

D. What does it mean?

A. What additional cross references or research do you need to do to understand the passage?

Part II. Class Notes and Discussion

Does additional evidence exist that Jesus claimed to be God?

Notes and Discussion

If Jesus claimed to be God, then could He have been just a good man?
Notes and Discussion

Reflections from C.S. Lewis and the trilemma

WHEATON PRESS
READ. RESPOND. REFLECT.

HUMAN

https://commons.wikimedia.org/wiki/File:Veronese_Hochzeit_zu_Kana.jpg

A wedding is celebrated in a courtyard surrounded by Dorian and Corinthian columns. The setting looks more like Veronese's 16th century Venice than like a city in Palestine.

According to the gospel of John, this is where Jesus performed the first of his seven miracles: he changed water into wine when the host ran out of supply.

Jesus is in the middle, next to his mother Mary. The two figures at the end of the table to the left are probably the bride and the groom. On the balustrade in the background, meat is being cut.

If it is lamb's meat, it could be a reference to the "Lamb of God," the name John the Baptist used for Jesus.

In the foreground sits a group of musicians. Some think that the man in the white gown is Veronese and that the man in red is Titian. Standing between them is an hourglass, a symbol of vanity.

A dog - symbol of loyalty - lies chewing on a bone.

To the right a man pours wine from a water jug. The two men behind him wonder at the water that has become wine.

Veronese painted this huge canvas commissioned by the monastery of San Giorgio Maggiore in Venice. It would hang there in the refectory for more than two centuries, until Napoleon robbed it and took it to Paris.

The work is one of the main attractions in the Louvre: it is in the same room as *Mona Lisa*.

During a restoration in 1992 it was damaged twice, first by dripping water and later when one of the supports gave way.

Fortunately the holes could be repaired by stitching the canvas back together.

Unit Essential Questions

1 Was Jesus fully human?

2 What do other religions believe about the humanity of Christ?

3 How does the full humanity of Christ influence my relationship with Jesus?

Unit Learning Objectives

A Examine other religions and worldviews to learn their perspective on the humanity of Christ

B Examine Scripture to discern if Jesus was fully human

C Evaluate historic and modern Gnosticism in light of the Epistles and church history

D Examine Christ's relationship with the Holy Spirit as the model of a normal life

Unit Learning Assessments

Unit exam

Daily Essential Questions

1 Was Jesus fully human?

2 What is Gnosticism?

3 What is the kenosis and why does it matter?

4 If Jesus was fully human, how could he live a perfect life?

What does it matter whether or not Jesus was fully human?

Notes and Discussion

What are some of the heresies regarding the humanity of Christ?

Notes and Discussion

Was Jesus fully human?
Small Group Project
  Passage study: 1 John 1, NASB

Introduction, the Incarnate Word

1 What was from the beginning, what we have heard, what we have seen with our eyes, what we have looked at and touched with our hands, concerning the Word of Life—

2 and the life was manifested, and we have seen and testify and proclaim to you the eternal life, which was with the Father and was manifested to us—

3 what we have seen and heard we proclaim to you also, so that you too may have fellowship with us; and indeed our fellowship is with the Father, and with His Son Jesus Christ.

4 These things we write, so that our joy may be made complete.

God Is Light

5 This is the message we have heard from Him and announce to you, that God is Light, and in Him there is no darkness at all.

6 If we say that we have fellowship with Him and yet walk in the darkness, we lie and do not practice the truth;

7 but if we walk in the Light as He Himself is in the Light, we have fellowship with one another, and the blood of Jesus His Son cleanses us from all sin.

8 If we say that we have no sin, we are deceiving ourselves and the truth is not in us.

9 If we confess our sins, He is faithful and righteous to forgive us our sins and to cleanse us from all unrighteousness.

10 If we say that we have not sinned, we make Him a liar and His word is not in us.

If Jesus was fully human, how could He live a perfect life?

Notes and Discussion

WHEATON PRESS
READ. RESPOND. REFLECT.

ATONEMENT

Who do you say I AM?

Mark 8:29

Unit Essential Questions

1   What physically happened to Jesus on the cross?

2   How does the cross of Christ fulfill the Old Testament requirements?

3   How are the perfect love and perfect wrath of God displayed through the cross of Christ?

Unit Learning Objectives

A   Examine and understand essential doctrinal definitions and their practical applications

B   Examine and articulate how Christ's death perfectly fulfills the Old Testament sacrificial system

C   Examine and articulate how the perfect love and perfect wrath of God is displayed through the cross of Christ

D   Examine the Scriptural evidence to determine if Christ ever went to hell after He died

Unit Learning Assessments

Gospel project appendix definitions

Love and wrath reflection paper

Atonement assessment

Daily Essential Questions

1   What physically happened to Christ on the cross?

2   What spiritually happened through the sacrifice of Christ on the cross?

3   What theologically happened through the atoning work of Christ?

4   How are the perfect love and perfect wrath of God fulfilled through the death of Christ on the cross?

5   Did Jesus go to hell after He died?

What physically happened to Jesus on the cross?

Notes and Discussion

What theologically happened through the atoning work of Christ?

Notes and Discussion

Name the seven essential truths to understanding the significance of Christ's death on the cross. **NOTE: you must state the references.

1.

2.

3.

4.

5.

6.

7.

What theologically happened through the atoning work of Christ?

Define the following doctrines and theological words:

1. Justification:

2. Sanctification:

3. Reconciliation:

4. Substitution:

5. Scapegoat:

6. Propitiation:

7. Day of Atonement:

Life of Christ

What theologically happened through the atoning work of Christ?

Define the following doctrines and theological words:

8. Penal substitutionary atonement:

9. Forbearance:

10. Expiation:

11. Atonement:

12. Imputation:

13. Glorification:

What theologically happened through the atoning work of Christ?

Short Answer

What are the three ways that Paul used the word saved in the New Testament?
(Identify the terms and their meanings.)

-

-

-

Did Jesus go to hell when He died?

1.

2.

3.

4.

5.

Did Jesus go to hell when He died?

Short Answer

Small group project

Reason 1.

Reason 2.

Reason 3.

Reason 4.

Reason 5.

Notes and Discussion

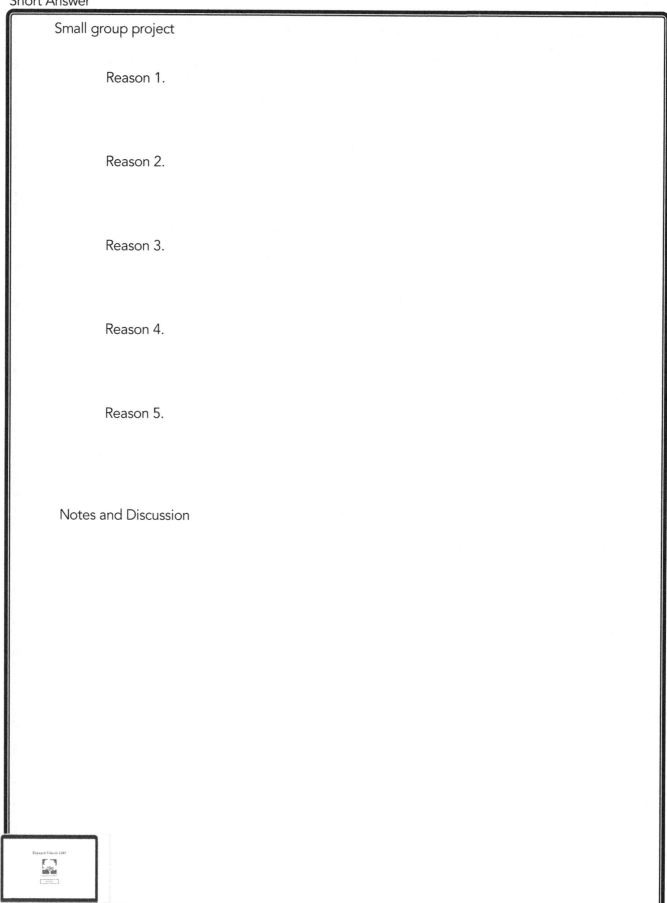

How did Christ's death fulfill the Old Testament sacrificial system?

Notes and Discussion

Jesus died for our sins, but what else did the cross accomplish?

Notes and Discussion

Practical Scenario I

A friend invites you to a local coffee shop and asks you the following question: "How is it fair that God can put both my really nice neighbor and Adolf Hitler side by side in hell?"

Using what you have learned in this unit, write out your response.

Notes and Discussion

Practical Scenario II

A friend invites you to a local coffee shop and asks you the following question: "How can a loving God send people to hell?"

Using what you have learned in this unit, write out your response.

Notes and Discussion

95

How are the perfect love and perfect wrath of God displayed through the cross of Christ?

Notes and Discussion

RISEN

Who do you say I AM?

Mark 8:29

Unit Essential Questions

1   What evidence exists that Jesus actually rose from the dead?

2   How does my perspective or conviction about the resurrection influence my relationship with Jesus?

Unit Learning Objectives

A   Examine the biblical evidence that Jesus rose from the dead

B   Examine the circumstantial evidence that Jesus rose from the dead

C   Examine the secular historical evidence that Jesus rose from the dead

D   Articulate a reasoned apologetic of personal beliefs regarding the resurrection of Christ

Unit Learning Assessments

9 Proofs project

9 Proofs reflection paper

Daily Essential Questions

1   What do I believe about the resurrection of Christ from the dead?

2   Is it reasonable to believe that Jesus rose from the dead?

3   What evidence exists that Jesus rose from the dead?

4   What do I believe is reasonable about the resurrection?

5   Can I articulate a clear apologetic for the resurrection of Christ from the dead?

Did Jesus rise from the dead?

- What do I believe about the resurrection of Christ?

- Why do I believe what I believe? (What proof or evidence is my belief based upon?)

- What does Jesus prove or accomplish through His resurrection?

- If Jesus did not rise from the dead, what would be the affect on modern Christianity?

Why does the resurrection of Christ matter?
Arguments from Scripture and logic

Notes and Discussion

Did Jesus rise from the dead?
What are the competing theories about the resurrection of Christ?

What is the biblical evidence for the resurrection of Christ?
Examining the biblical evidence

Directions: Summarize each of the nine pieces of biblical evidence for the resurrection of Christ. Include at least one Scripture reference within each summary.

1.

2.

3.

4.

What is the biblical evidence for the resurrection of Christ?
Examining the biblical evidence

Directions: Summarize each of the nine pieces of biblical evidence for the resurrection of Christ. Include at least one Scripture reference within each summary.

5.

6.

7.

8.

9.

What is the circumstantial evidence for the resurrection of Christ?

Examining the circumstantial evidence

Directions: Summarize each of the ten pieces of circumstantial evidence by answering all of the following three questions:

    A. What is the claim?
    B. Why is the claim significant?
    C. How does the claim give credible evidence for an argument?

1.
    A.

    B.

    C.

2.
    A.

    B.

    C.

3.
    A.

    B.

    C.

4.
    A.

    B.

    C.

5.
    A.

    B.

    C.

What is the circumstantial evidence for the resurrection of Christ?
Examining the circumstantial evidence

5.

    A.

    B.

    C.

6.

    A.

    B.

    C.

7.

    A.

    B.

    C.

8.

    A.

    B.

    C.

9.

    A.

    B.

    C.

10.

    A.

    B.

    C.

What is the secular historical evidence for the resurrection of Christ?
Examining the secular historical evidence

Directions: Summarize each of the pieces of secular historical evidence for the resurrection of Christ.

1.

2.

3.

4.

What do I find to be the most reasonable evidence for the resurrection?

What do I believe? Why do I believe it?

Directions:

From your perspective, what are the three most reasonable pieces of evidence in each category?

What is my biblical evidence for the resurrection of Christ?

1.

2.

3.

What is my circumstantial evidence for the resurrection of Christ?

1.

2.

3.

What is the secular historical evidence for the resurrection of Christ?

1.

2.

3.

Nine proofs for the resurrection of Christ

What do I believe? Why do I believe it?

Assessment:

Directions: Answer the following question in a well–formatted, five paragraph answer.
Each paragraph must have a minimum of four sentences. The first paragraph should be a well
crafted introduction, and the last paragraph should be a smoothly articulated conclusion.

Question: Based on biblical, historical, secular, and circumstantial evidence, did Jesus die and rise
from the dead?

Gospel Check Insights
Notes and Discussion

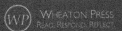

RETURN

Who do you say I am? Mark 8:29

Unit Essential Questions

1   How does the life of Christ fit into the eternal plan of God?

2   What does the Bible tell us about the return of Christ?

3   Where is Jesus now, and what will He do when He returns?

4   How does my perspective of Christ's return influence my relationship with Christ and others?

Unit Learning Objectives

A   Examine what the Bible says about the current and future ministry of Christ

B   Examine primary orthodox perspectives on the return of Christ

C   Understand the significance of modern events in light of biblical prophecy regarding Christ's return

D   Examine my role in the eternal mission of God in light of the return of Christ

Unit Learning Assessments

Theological position paper

Daily Essential Questions

1   How does the life of Christ fit into the eternal plan of God?

2   Where is Jesus now?

3   How does the return of Christ fit into the eternal plan of God?

4   What will He do when He returns?

5   How should my beliefs affect my current life?

Bell Ringers

Directions: Answer the following questions based on your opinion and understanding of Scripture.

1. Where is Jesus today?

2. What Scripture do you have to support your answer for question 1?

3. Is Jesus reigning as king today? (Why or why not?)

4. What Scripture do you have to support your answer for 3?

5. What are the implications of your answers to these questions?

Where is Jesus today?
Research project

Directions:

Find a partner. Each partner should summarize five of the ten statements with two or three bullet points. When finished, combine your lists to create a complete list of ten, which you will utilize as a study guide for this unit.

**NOTE: your summaries need to contain answers to the following three questions:

- What does the Bible teach (and what do I believe about the subject)?

- Why should I, or do I, believe this? (What references or Scriptural evidence do I base my belief upon?)

- So what? What are the implications of this belief for my life?

    1.

    2.

    3.

Where is Jesus today?
Research project

4.

5.

6.

7.

Where is Jesus today?
Research project

8.

9.

10.

What will Jesus do upon His return?
Research project

Directions:

Find a partner. Each partner should summarize five of the ten statements with 2 or 3 bullet points. When finished, combine your lists to create a complete list of 10, which you will utilize as a study guide for this unit.

**NOTE: your summaries need to contain the answers to the following three questions:

- What does the Bible teach (and what do I believe about the subject)?

- Why should I, or do I, believe this? (What references or Scriptural evidence do I base my belief upon?)

- So what? What are the implications of this belief on my life?

1.

2.

3.

What will Jesus do upon His return?
Research project

4.

5.

6.

7.

What will Jesus do upon His return?
Research project

8.

9.

10.

What will happen when Jesus returns?
Revelation 21–22, NASB

The New Heaven and Earth

1 Then I saw a new heaven and a new earth; for the first heaven and the first earth passed away, and there is no longer any sea. 2 And I saw the holy city, new Jerusalem, coming down out of heaven from God, made ready as a bride adorned for her husband. 3 And I heard a loud voice from the throne, saying, "Behold, the tabernacle of God is among men, and He will dwell among them, and they shall be His people, and God Himself will be among them, 4 and He will wipe away every tear from their eyes; and there will no longer be any death; there will no longer be any mourning, or crying, or pain; the first things have passed away."

5 And He who sits on the throne said, "Behold, I am making all things new." And He *said, "Write, for these words are faithful and true." 6 Then He said to me, "It is done. I am the Alpha and the Omega, the beginning and the end. I will give to the one who thirsts from the spring of the water of life without cost. 7 He who overcomes will inherit these things, and I will be his God and he will be My son. 8 But for the cowardly and unbelieving and abominable and murderers and immoral persons and sorcerers and idolaters and all liars, their part will be in the lake that burns with fire and brimstone, which is the second death."

9 Then one of the seven angels who had the seven bowls full of the seven last plagues came and spoke with me, saying, "Come here, I will show you the bride, the wife of the Lamb."

What will happen when Jesus returns?
Revelation 21–22, NASB

The New Jerusalem

10 And he carried me away in the Spirit to a great and high mountain, and showed me the holy city, Jerusalem, coming down out of heaven from God, 11 having the glory of God. Her brilliance was like a very costly stone, as a stone of crystal–clear jasper. 12 It had a great and high wall, with twelve gates, and at the gates twelve angels; and names were written on them, which are the names of the twelve tribes of the sons of Israel. 13 There were three gates on the east and three gates on the north and three gates on the south and three gates on the west. 14 And the wall of the city had twelve foundation stones, and on them were the twelve names of the twelve apostles of the Lamb.

15 The one who spoke with me had a gold measuring rod to measure the city, and its gates and its wall. 16 The city is laid out as a square, and its length is as great as the width; and he measured the city with the rod, fifteen hundred miles; its length and width and height are equal. 17 And he measured its wall, seventy–two yards, according to human measurements, which are also angelic measurements. 18 The material of the wall was jasper; and the city was pure gold, like clear glass. 19 The foundation stones of the city wall were adorned with every kind of precious stone. The first foundation stone was jasper; the second, sapphire; the third, chalcedony; the fourth, emerald; 20 the fifth, sardonyx; the sixth, sardius; the seventh, chrysolite; the eighth, beryl; the ninth, topaz; the tenth, chrysoprase; the eleventh, jacinth; the twelfth, amethyst. 21 And the twelve gates were twelve pearls; each one of the gates was a single pearl. And the street of the city was pure gold, like transparent glass.

What will happen when Jesus returns?
Revelation 21–22, NASB

22 I saw no temple in it, for the Lord God the Almighty and the Lamb are its temple. 23 And the city has no need of the sun or of the moon to shine on it, for the glory of God has illumined it, and its lamp is the Lamb. 24 The nations will walk by its light, and the kings of the earth will bring their glory into it. 25 In the daytime (for there will be no night there) its gates will never be closed; 26 and they will bring the glory and the honor of the nations into it; 27 and nothing unclean, and no one who practices abomination and lying, shall ever come into it, but only those whose names are written in the Lamb's book of life.

The River and the Tree of Life

1 Then he showed me a river of the water of life, clear as crystal, coming from the throne of God and of the Lamb, 2 in the middle of its street. On either side of the river was the tree of life, bearing twelve kinds of fruit, yielding its fruit every month; and the leaves of the tree were for the healing of the nations. 3 There will no longer be any curse; and the throne of God and of the Lamb will be in it, and His bond–servants will serve Him; 4 they will see His face, and His name will be on their foreheads. 5 And there will no longer be any night; and they will not have need of the light of a lamp nor the light of the sun, because the Lord God will illumine them; and they will reign forever and ever.

6 And he said to me, "These words are faithful and true"; and the Lord, the God of the spirits of the prophets, sent His angel to show to His bond–servants the things which must soon take place.

7 "And behold, I am coming quickly. Blessed is he who heeds the words of the prophecy of this book."

What will happen when Jesus returns?
Revelation 21–22, NASB

8 I, John, am the one who heard and saw these things. And when I heard and saw, I fell down to worship at the feet of the angel who showed me these things. 9 But he *said to me, "Do not do that. I am a fellow servant of yours and of your brethren the prophets and of those who heed the words of this book. Worship God."

The Final Message

10 And he *said to me, "Do not seal up the words of the prophecy of this book, for the time is near. 11 Let the one who does wrong, still do wrong; and the one who is filthy, still be filthy; and let the one who is righteous, still practice righteousness; and the one who is holy, still keep himself holy."

12 "Behold, I am coming quickly, and My reward is with Me, to render to every man according to what he has done. 13 I am the Alpha and the Omega, the first and the last, the beginning and the end."

14 Blessed are those who wash their robes, so that they may have the right to the tree of life, and may enter by the gates into the city. 15 Outside are the dogs and the sorcerers and the immoral persons and the murderers and the idolaters, and everyone who loves and practices lying.

16 "I, Jesus, have sent My angel to testify to you these things for the churches. I am the root and the descendant of David, the bright morning star."

17 The Spirit and the bride say, "Come." And let the one who hears say, "Come." And let the one who is thirsty come; let the one who wishes take the water of life without cost.

What will happen when Jesus returns?
Revelation 21–22, NASB

18 I testify to everyone who hears the words of the prophecy of this book: if anyone adds to them, God will add to him the plagues which are written in this book; 19 and if anyone takes away from the words of the book of this prophecy, God will take away his part from the tree of life and from the holy city, which are written in this book.

20 He who testifies to these things says, "Yes, I am coming quickly." Amen. Come, Lord Jesus.

21 The grace of the Lord Jesus be with all. Amen.

Assessment of learning
Doctrine position paper

There are three stages for this assessment.

1. Formative stage: This is the first draft of your position paper. It will not be graded but will demonstrate your learning progression and process.

2. Summative assessment: This is the final draft of your position paper. It is graded and will demonstrate what you have learned.
   **NOTE: Your last copy of a position paper becomes your summative assessment grade.

3. Student-initiated assessment: This demonstration of higher learning is initiated at any time during the process by a student who resubmits a formative position paper to demonstrate a higher level of learning. This ensures that throughout the process, learning is the constant and time is the variable.

Summative grading. Learning objectives in the WHAT and WHY sections of the paper will be based on this scale of proficiency:

1	2	3	4
Demonstrates little (if any) knowledge or understanding of material explicitly taught in class. Zero to 50% of statements are backed up by outside references.	Demonstrates basic knowledge or understanding of material explicitly taught in class. 50% to 75% of statements are backed up by references.	Demonstrates knowledge or understanding of material explicitly taught in class and includes material explicitly taught in the course textbook. 75% to 90% of statements are backed up by references.	Demonstrates level 3 knowledge and understanding and includes material pulled from additional outside academic/theological resources or demonstrates higher–level critical thinking by connecting specific doctrines to other essential learning outcomes, essential questions, or doctrines. 90–100% of statements are backed up by outside references and sources.

0	1	2
Not Attempted	Student demonstrates a generic or simplistic application. Sentences or thoughts are not complete. Responses do not meet the minimum of four sentences for a complete paragraph. Student demonstrates basic (if any) interaction with the material in a personal way. Thoughts are generic or incomplete in nature.	Evidence is given that the student interacted with the significance of their beliefs in a meaningful way. References are made to how his or her beliefs or apologetic affect his or her life and demonstrate higher–level thought, critical thinking, and personal reflection. Thoughts are complete and demonstrate an interaction with the material in paragraphs of at least four sentences.

Assessment of learning
Doctrine position paper

Summative grading:

For every learning objective, you will be assessed on what you <u>know</u>, <u>understand</u>, and <u>do</u> (K.U.D.) as a result of your interaction with the material. Each position paper will assess three areas of learning through a What?, Why?, and So What? section in your paper.

1. What? (doctrinal understanding)

    This section is a demonstration of what you <u>know</u> to be true (40%).

    Every sentence in this section must contain a reference. References are what separate an opinion paper from a position paper.

    Each sentence should contain the words "I believe" followed by a statement of your beliefs, then followed by a reference.

2. Why? (doctrinal apologetic)

    This section is a demonstration of your <u>understanding</u> of the reason that you believe (see 1 Peter 3:15) (40%).

    While many of the sentences in this section will contain references, it is not mandatory that all of them contain references.

    Sentences should contain the words "I believe (restatement of belief) because…" followed by the reason you find your belief to be reasonable. You cannot state that you believe something "because the Bible says so" because you are taking a position on why you have reached your conclusion.

3. So What? (practical application)

    This section is a demonstration of what you will <u>do</u> to apply your knowledge and understanding to your life beyond the classroom (20%).

    This section should be a reflection of your personality and writing style.

RESPOND

Unit Essential Questions

1 What is worship?

2 What is my response to Jesus?

3 How will I articulate what I have learned to others?

Unit Learning Objectives

A Articulate a personalized response to Christ's question, "Who do others say that I am?"

B Articulate a personalized response to Christ's question, "Who do you say that I am?"

Unit Learning Assessments

Gospel project

Final presentation

Final exam

Daily Essential Questions

1 What is the meaning of worship?

2 What functional saviors compete for prominence in my life?

3 What will be my response to the invitation of Christ?

4 How will I articulate what I have learned?

Reflection

Take some time to reflect on what you have been learning.

1. What has God been teaching me?

2. What have I learned through this process?

3. What is one surprise I've had?

4. What is one thing that stands out to me where I can see growth in my life?

5. What is one area where I would like to see more growth between now and the end of the semester?

1.

How will I respond?
Notes and Dialogue

1.   What is worship?

2.   Who or what do I glorify through my life and actions?

3.   What makes Jesus superior to other saviors? Who or what do I trust to save me?

4.   What is my response to Jesus?

What is a functional savior?
Notes and Dialogue

How do functional saviors manifest themselves in my life?
Personal reflection

Illustrating my story

"To them God has chosen to make known among the Gentiles the glorious riches of this mystery, which is Christ in you, the hope of glory."

Colossians 1:27

"I am The Way, The Truth, and The Life."

John 14:6

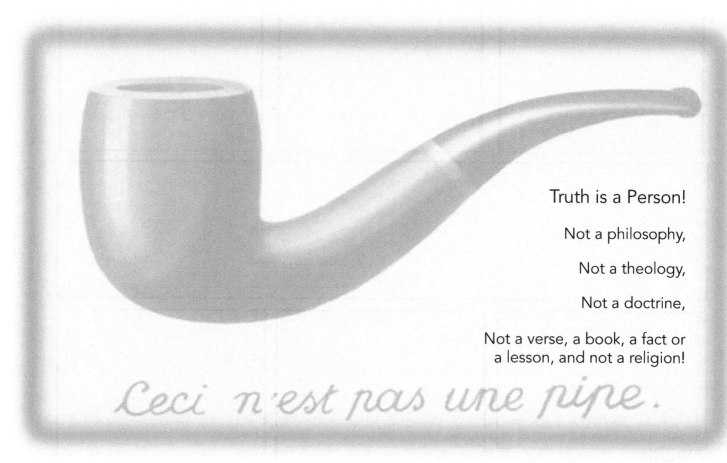

Truth is a Person!

Not a philosophy,

Not a theology,

Not a doctrine,

Not a verse, a book, a fact or a lesson, and not a religion!

Ceci n'est pas une pipe.

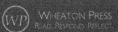

RESOURCES

How to Write a One–Page Paper for Bible Class

It is not enough to simply memorize Bible facts or acquire biblical knowledge. Students need to be given the opportunity to wrestle with important issues, develop personal beliefs, and articulate those beliefs in clear and convincing ways, in both written and oral form. At our school, we value the ability to think critically and communicate clearly about theological truth. It is the belief of the Bible Department that Bible class offers the opportunity to practice and develop these skills through the medium of one–page papers.

One–page papers are made up of a centered title and four critical paragraphs. The first part of the paper is referred to as the "hook" paragraph, and it is used to relate the topic to the audience. The second part of the paper is the "book" paragraph. The purpose of this paragraph is to clearly state the main concept of the paper. The third paragraph is the "look" paragraph, and it is where the writer illustrates the main point he or she has outlined in the second paragraph. The fourth and final section is called the "took" paragraph. It is in this final paragraph that the writer outlines a personal application, lesson, or "take away" from the topic.

Each individual paragraph must also contain a few key elements. One of the key elements is that each paragraph needs a minimum of four sentences. Another key element is that each paragraph needs to include transition sentences and be double–spaced. The paper should be written using either eleven- or twelve-point Times New Roman or Arial font. Finally, while the paper itself will using APA guidelines, it is important to note that the paper must not be longer than one page in total length (Bible Reference 1:1).

There are three main things you will accomplish through these papers. First, you will critically examine your personal beliefs. Second, you will learn how to communicate your beliefs in concise written form. Third and finally, you will have a collection of papers outlining your beliefs, which you can use for personal reference in the future.

Student Name
Class, Period
Date

Commentary on _____ (name of Gospel)

Chapter 1

Write a one-paragraph synopsis or reflection on each chapter. Each paragraph should include a single line identifying the chapter (see above). Each paragraph should start at least one space after the chapter heading, and each paragraph should have at least four sentences. Reflections on the passage could include summaries, devotional journal entries, or references to specific verses. If you reference a verse, do not quote the verse verbatim; instead, summarize or personalize the context or meaning and include an APA style reference at the end of the sentence (Gospel 1:1).

Chapter 2

Write a one-paragraph synopsis or reflection on each chapter. Each paragraph should include a single line identifying the chapter (see above). Each paragraph should start at least one space after the chapter heading, and each paragraph should have at least four sentences. Reflections on the passage could include summaries, devotional journal entries, or references to specific verses. If you reference a verse, do not quote the verse verbatim; instead, summarize or personalize the context or meaning and include an APA style reference at the end of the sentence (Gospel 1:1).

Chapter 3

Write a one-paragraph synopsis or reflection on each chapter. Each paragraph should include a single line identifying the chapter (see above). Each paragraph should start at least one space after the chapter heading, and each paragraph should have at least four sentences. Reflections on the passage could include summaries, devotional journal entries, or references to specific verses. If you reference a verse, do not quote the verse verbatim; instead, summarize or personalize the context or meaning and include an APA style reference at the end of the sentence (Gospel 1:1).

135

Gospel Project
Table of Contents

Table of Contents

Assessment Socratic Dialogue
How will I be graded?

Standard	Element not present for assessment	Does not meet standard	Meets standard at basic level	Above average in standard	Proficient in standard
	1	2	3	4	5
Conduct	Arrives unprepared without notes, pencil/pen, or perhaps even without the text.	Displays little respect for the learning process. Argumentative or apathetic. Takes advantage of minor distractions. Uses inappropriate language. Speaks to individuals rather than ideas. Arrives unprepared without notes, pencil/pen, or perhaps even without the text.	Participates and expresses a belief that his/her ideas are important in understanding the text. May make insightful comments, but does not contribute to the progress of the conversation.	Generally shows composure, but may display impatience with contradictory or confusing ideas. Comments, but does not necessarily encourage others to participate.	Demonstrates respect for the learning process. Has patience with different opinions and complexity of ideas. Shows initiative by asking others for clarification. Brings others into the conversation. Moves the conversation forward. Speaks to all of the participants. Avoids talking too much.
Speaking and reasoning	Arrives unprepared without notes, pencil/pen, or perhaps even without the text.	Extremely reluctant to participate even when called upon. Comments are illogical and meaningless. May mumble or express incomplete ideas. Little or no account taken of previous comments or important ideas in the text.	Responds to questions but may have to be called upon by others. Has read the text but not put much effort into preparing questions and ideas for the seminar. Comments take details into account but may not flow logically in conversation.	Responds to questions voluntarily. Comments show an appreciation for the text. Comments are logical, but not connected to other speakers. Ideas interesting enough that others respond.	Understands questions asked before answering them. Cites evidence from text. Expresses thoughts in complete sentences. Moves conversation forward. Makes connections between ideas.
Listening	Arrives unprepared without notes, pencil/pen, or perhaps even without the text.	Appears uninvolved in the seminar. Comments display complete misinterpretation of questions or comments of other participants.	Appears to find some ideas unimportant while responding to others. May require questions or confusions to be repeated due to inattention. Takes few notes during the seminar in response to ideas and comments.	Generally pays attention and responds thoughtfully to ideas and questions of other participants and the leader. Absorption in own ideas may distract the participant from the ideas of others.	Pays attention to details. Writes down questions. Responses take into account all participants. Demonstrates that he/she has kept up. Points out faulty logic respectfully. Overcomes distractions.
Critical reading	Arrives unprepared without notes, pencil/pen, or perhaps even without the text.	Student is unprepared for the seminar. Important words, phrases, and/or ideas in the text are unfamiliar. No notes or questions are marked in the text. No attempt made to get help with difficult material.	Appears to have read or skimmed the text, but has not marked the text or made meaningful notes or questions. Little evidence of serious reflection prior to the seminar.	Has read the text and comes with some ideas from it, but these may not be written out in advance. Occasionally references terms and page numbers.	Thoroughly familiar with the text. Has notations and questions in the margins (when applicable). Key words, phrases, and ideas are highlighted. Possible contradictions are identified. Uses terms and page numbers where appropriate.

How will I be Graded?
Grading standard and proficiency rubric

PRESENTATION RUBRIC			
	Below Standard	Approaching Standard	At Standard	Above Standard
Explanation of Ideas, Information and Content	• Too few, inappropriate, or irrelevant descriptions, facts, details, or examples to clearly explain ideas or content	• Uses some descriptions, facts, and details but some may be irrelevant or there may still be an inadequate amount	• Uses relevant, well-chosen descriptions, facts, details, and examples to support claims and to address the Driving Question	
Organization and Clarity	• Does not address Driving Question or include require content in the presentation • Does not organize content in a manner that provides clarity or makes sense • Does not have an introduction or conclusion • Uses time poorly or the presentation is too long or too short	• Includes nearly all criteria outlined in the Driving Question or presentation rubric • Some content is organized and makes sense but other parts seem out of order or lack organization • Introduction and conclusion exist but do not add value to the presentation • Overall timing is within limits but may spend too much or too little time on an idea or visual aid	• Includes all criteria outlined in the Driving Question or presentation rubric • Moves clearly through the presentation with ideas and concepts building naturally • Introduction and conclusion is effective • Time is well organized, and presentation is not rushed or long	
Eye Contact, Body Language and voice	• Does not look at audience • Reads notes or slides • Does not use gestures or movements • Lacks poise (fidgets, slouches) • Mumbles or speaks too softly • Inappropriate or informal language (slang)	• Infrequent eye contact, reads notes or slides most of the time • Some gestures or movements • Demonstrates some poise and confidence with minimal fidgeting • Speaks clearing most of the time • Occasionally uses "filler words"	• Speaks clearly and makes frequent eye contact • Changes tone when appropriate • Rarely uses "filler words" • Uses natural gestures and movements	
Visual Aids	• Does not use visual aids or visual is distracting	• Some visual aides are distracting or do not add value to the presentation	• Well produced and created visual aides that clarify information adding value and interest	
Response to Questions	• Does not address audience questions or interact with audience	• Some audience interaction but not always clearly or completely	• Clear and intentional audience interaction • Able to admit when they do not know an answer but can offer a possible solution of where to look	

An invitation to transformation
Personal Application

1. Reflect: What has God revealed to you through this process?

2. Respond: What is He asking you to do about it?

3. Reproduce: What steps do you need to take, and who do you need to talk to next?

Sign your name and add the date to remind you of your commitment.
Keep it in a place where it will remind you to take your next steps.

Name: _____ Date: _____

Follow me, I will make you fishers of men....

Jesus

Made in the USA
Middletown, DE
12 September 2019